AND THE OHANA CONTINUES

And the Ohana Continues

Herman D. Lujan, Ph.D.

Copyright © 2017 by Herman D. Lujan, Ph.D.

Memior

Pictures are taken from family albums.

ISBN: Softcover   9781645505372

All rights reserved. No part of this book may be reproduced or transmitted in any form or by any means, electronic or mechanical, including photocopying, recording, or by any information storage and retrieval system, without permission in writing from the copyright owner.

Lujan Foreword

This story that needs to be told is a documentary glimpse of Hawaii's historic role in melding diverse ethnicities in a remarkably synergistic way. The descending generations of a marriage between a native Hawaiian Spaniard and a stoic Azorean woman of Hawaiian birth, were gifted with the finest qualities of each parental resource.

More than synergistic, the combined ethnic and cultural admixture was expressed in prepotency, the inherent predisposition to pass on one's qualities to succeeding generations. Credit goes to the Azorean, Iberian and Marquesan forebears of the Lujan and Ignacio 'ohana.

With the marriage of patriarchal Spaniard Lucas Lujan and Kaililau Palea, whose genealogy is blue blooded, a brood of thirteen children were born. Samuel Hoolohekamohoalii was the ninth born (1894). His birthplace was Peleau, ancestral lands of the Palea line of po'e kahiko located on the eastern slopes of Mauna Kea in the district of North Hilo.

In neighboring Hāmākua, a child was born to Amos Joaquin Ignacio and his wife Augusta, both immigrants from the Azores. Alice Pauline Ignacio was the first of ten children born of this union.

The marriage of Sam Lujan and Alice Ignacio launched a five decade expression of fundamental values of aloha for the 'ohana and

ʻāina underscored by education as the means of enhancing the lives of their children, grand children and great-grandchildren.

Sam and Alice were exemplary in expressing that achievement of education, professional and social skills as well as the comforts of home that came by way of personal sacrifice. They were blessed with Kenneth, Herman (Leilehua), and Alice (Leilani). who were gifted with parents who set a high bar of achievement for them. Sam was knowledgeable in ranching and farming while Alice's progressive role in public education reached historic proportions. They epitomized the Hawaiian values of aloha, while embracing the land's magnetism as the basis of ʻohana.

I am honored to compose the foreword for this work that goes far beyond the value of inspiring generations of youth to kū lia i ka nuʻu, strive for the highest, through educational pursuits. This documentary is an expression of gratitude for one's parents and ancestral lineage , a pau loa.

My relationship with the Lujan family spans many decades beginning as a country boy whose parents and sisters held the Lujan family in high regard. Especially memorable were the Sunday afternoons our families spent together visiting in the spacious two-story Lujan ranch home. Even then, my interests were of the outdoors—browsing in Sam's vineyards (sour grapes), manicured orchards (sweet oranges), and afternoon highlights visiting his paddocks of fine cattle, sturdy corrals and secure fences bordered by tall eucalyptus trees.

While a student at St. Joseph's School in Hilo where I was several years behind Herman and Leilani, I was readily impressed with the natural leadership roles the Lujan children held. Herman was versatile—reciting poetry before the student body or as a thespian in theatrical performances. Both he and Alice were gifted with splendid voices whether in choir, church or classroom venues. Considered by all as "Spanish Hawaiians" the Lujan children were a credit to their heritage, school and faith.

Parental sacrifice was genuine for the senior Lujan's as Herman and Leilani went off to college on the mainland earning doctoral degrees in their respective fields. Herman's stature as President of the University of Northern Colorado at Greeley is an historic achievement in the context of Hawaiian progress. Leilani's excellence in the field of education at the California State University San Marcos is equally noteworthy in her enduring quest to educate young men and women who need to "come from behind" to achieve academic excellence.

Speaking for the Bergin 'ohana, the senior Lujan's exemplified parenthood of the finest order. I can safely attest to the fact that the communities of the Big Island watched with pride over the half-century fruit of Lujan influence—a Spanish Hawaiian Legacy.

This book is a must read for the youth of Hawai'i, especially those that feel overwhelmed with challenges to forward progress in self-enrichment and empowerment.

Do it the Lujan way—stand firm in the face of adversity but lean forward to meet the challenges.

Dr. Billy Bergin

Contents

Lujan Foreword v

Preface xiii
    This is a story of a family and its land and the struggle for survival it experiences.

Prologue xv
    ʻĀina (land) and ʻohana (family) are the centerpieces of the Hawaiian survival story from ancient times to the present.

Chapter One: The Landing 1
    The arrival of the Spanish Cabin Boy and the marriage to his Hawaiian wife mark the beginning of the Lujan ʻohana.

Chapter Two: The Countryside 6
    Lujan is taken by the countryside and its economy.

Chapter Three: The Family 9
    The Lujan ʻohana grows, and Lujan moves the family to Kaililau's ancestral land, where the ʻohana encounters a Portuguese family engaged in education and teaching in local schools.

Chapter Four: The Uncommon Alliance..27

The designated next leader of the Lujan ʻohana marries the eldest daughter of the Portuguese family, and together they turn education into their vessel of survival for the ʻohana. The role of women emerges as a key asset in preparing the emerging new leadership of the ʻohana.

Chapter Five: The Blight 35

Pestilence, lack of skills in sugar technology, lack of education, and the role of religion combine to decimate Hawaiians physically and spiritually.

Chapter Six: Shaping Change 41

The resulting changes in sugar technology and other modernizations take the land and the native culture away. The Lujan family is hit by pestilence. Six members of the Lujan ʻohana of thirteen die young. The immortality and economics of poverty that follow behind them are papered over by religion and the facade of democracy.

Chapter Seven: The State...48

The Second World War hits Hawaiʻi hard. Changes in the postwar economy and society profoundly affect Hawaiians and their lifestyle. Alice Pauline gets her Master of Arts degree in speech and reading from Barnard College in New York and rises in her role in the ʻohana. Hawaiʻi is annexed.

Chapter Eight: From Sickle to Blade..63

Samuel Hoʻolohekamohoaliʻi brings new technologies to the ʻohana farming and ranching endeavors.

Chapter Nine: Connections..77
    Connections with individuals and groups enrich life and are a resource to the 'ohana personally and professionally.

Chapter Ten: The Influencers 103
    What it is like to live in an in-between world. Finding the wisdom and learning in stories and conversation. Learning from the *kupuna* (elders).

Chapter Eleven: The Learned and Good Person 144
    Understanding what makes a good and learned person.

Chapter Twelve: Sweet Home 150
    The keys to a good life are being part of a living 'ohana, preserving what you learn in a changing world, and passing it on to the 'ohana.

Chapter Thirteen: For the Children.. 156
    Passing on the culture.

Epilogue 165
Acknowledgements.. 171

Preface

In a pluralistic and global world, there are many untold stories of ordinary indigenous people who have chosen to remain resilient in spite of national policies determined to Americanize, assimilate, and acculturate those who are "different." Nurtured by inner strength, by a strong sense of their own realities, and by an extraordinary vision fed by unique creativity that only knew limitless possibilities, kanakas saw themselves not as heroes but as everyday people who worked hard to make the best life they possibly could for themselves and their families. Self-pity had no place in their consciousness. Their actions were principled. They remained focused on their families, supporting them without question and loving them unconditionally. In the face of oppression, they remained proud and knowledgeable about their roots, their cultures, their heritages, and their determination to be well grounded, never losing their sense of self.

This book offers one of many untold stories. It is the story of an indigenous Hawaiian family whose personal histories are deeply rooted in the past, populated by multicultural influences, a whirl of life-changing events, and the need to look back into the past to make sense of what it means to be indigenous in a modern world that seeks to charm individuals to think like others and dilute their individual sense of personal identity.

This story begins before Hawai'i was a state or even a territory. The book tells the story to a younger generation to remind them that Hawaiians—though they now are people of diverse heritage—came from proud traditions and beliefs that the land was everything, was preserved in righteousness, and would take care of everyone forever. That sense of endurance is what sustained the 'ohana, a word used loosely in modern days to talk about a group with common interests. But traditionally for Hawaiians and for the family whose story is told in this book, 'ohana goes way beyond that. It is blood, connection, tradition, emotional similarities, and a constant struggle to endure even when precious rights are taken away—just as the land was taken from many Hawaiians. There is a strength that says trying again one more time is just what we do for the 'ohana, for the 'aina.

This is a story that needs to be told. It shares a rich heritage through the eyes of ordinary people deeply affected by change, and in doing so, it reminds the young people that change does not have to remake a person into someone else. It is possible to have feet in both worlds. It is possible to be a full participant in the microculture from which one came without betrayal of who a person is in the macroworld and global society. To help our readers understand the context of this heartfelt story, the prologue explains two driving concepts: the 'aina and the 'ohana.

Prologue

Two underlying concepts leap from the pages of Hawaiian history. They are 'aina and 'ohana. 'Aina is more than land—it is the land that feeds (*ai*). 'Ohana is not just people—it is the people together in a community that nourishes and shares both food and a spiritual sense of belonging that is deeper than what people call *aloha*. It is righteousness, a moral sense of doing things right (*pono*). Together, these two elements—land and family—are the cornerstones of being Hawaiian.

The people of *kahiko* (ancestors) were seamen of the first order from the Marquesas Islands. These Marquesans settled and used the nearby islands for shelter and food. As they grew, they often forayed across the many islands of the South Pacific on fishing and food gathering expeditions. Their navigational skills led them into further unknown waters, in search of new sources of food and shelter. On one of these trips, they sighted land that turned out to be the island of Kaua'i. They ventured from Kaua'i and landed at Ka Lae (South Point) on the island of Hawai'i. As they wandered across the cape of Ka Lae, they found the lush plains of Kau, shielded by the tall forest stands of koa and sandalwood. The plains on the lower slopes provided food to sustain them as they began to settle in. The *kalo* (taro) and its corm gave them what they needed for making *poi*, their staple. The two dozen or so other canoe plants they brought with them included *kukui* (candlenut), *ulu* (breadfruit), *niu* (coconut), *olena* (turmeric), *uala* (sweet potato), *mai'a* (banana), *ko* (sugarcane), and *awapuhi* (ginger). The loamy plains nurtured other edibles as well. Finally, this 'aina (land) was a better place than the one they called home.

Kanakas, as we call ourselves, are a people who brought their social system along with them on the voyages to the new lands. Known as the *kapu*, it was a system of values that guided communities as they came together. It was a code of rules to live by that held families and communities together.

The land use pattern at home was called *ahupua'a*, and its potential application in the new land made it clear that while they should return home, they should consider returning to the new great islands they had found. It took two years or so to rebuild and service their fleet. Then like the Conestoga wagons of the westward expansion in the mainland US exploration, the canoes were the vessels they would use for their future expeditions.

They arrived home to celebration and the storytelling of their adventure. They described the new islands as vast and open to revisits and settlement. In time, new expeditions and island settlement became realities. They set sail with food to plant, animals to eat, and tools to build their ahupua'a in this place called Hawai'i. The rest is modern history. Captain Cook's discovery came in 1778. By 1820, missionaries had come and became the barons of the new economy. In 1848, the Great Mahele came, dividing the lands roughly in thirds—one-third to the king, one-third to the chiefs (*ali'i*), and the remainder to the common people. Land itself, under a chief, was divided into districts (*moku*). Subunits were called *ili* and were overseen by *konohiki*, who were the lead land use officials under the ali'i. Land was distributed by Royal Patent Grants through the use of quit claim deeds.

The economy of sandalwood traded for Chinese cloth atrophied quickly as the supply of trees rapidly declined. This made land for other uses an asset to the shift in trade. Ranching and sugar production would displace the ahupua'a. Disease would decimate the kanakas. New technology would undermine the economic value of the kanakas as *paniolo* (cowboys) and laborers, but even these options were fading by the time annexation was proclaimed as the bringing of democracy to the little kingdom in the Pacific. Queen Lili'uokalani was forced to abdicate on January 17, 1893. A US gunship anchored in the bay across the street from Iolani Palace, a cannon was moved on the land and aimed at the palace, and US Marines faced off against the tiny royal guard of forty police armed with small arms and rifles. The change from kingdom to so-called democracy took place at the point of a gun. In July 1894, Samuel Ho'olohekamohoali'i Lucas Lujan was born, and the story of his 'ohana begins.

Chapter One

The Landing

Ho'omaka

It was a bright sunny day. The English trading ship was adjusting her sails to the brisk Kona winds. It was morning, so the incoming trade winds nudged her toward the Ho'okena wharf. The captain had her tacking just right. He had done this many times, so for him, this was just another sunlit day in Kona. Or was it?

The captain chatted this morning with his cabin boy who now had more than twenty years on the seas, keeping the captain's books, taking care of the captain's personal effects, and writing and translating business documents. A speaker of English and Spanish, Lucas Lujan Sr. left home at age nine in 1854. Over the years, Lucas had become a favorite among the cabin boys that the captain had employed in his many years running a route from Spain to China. The journey began in Spain, tacking toward the Ladrone Islands in the South China Sea, then slipping around the southern tip of Tierra del Fuego in South America to the cape in the South China Sea, and heading full speed to Hawai'i before finally docking in China. The ship always carried European goods in its cargo and Hawai'i sandalwood and food to China. In its return trip, the ship bore Chinese merchandise and silk back to Europe. The stops in Hawai'i and the Ladrones were especially necessary to get fruits and other food that staved off the sailor's disease, scurvy.

The Ladrones were discovered by Magellan in 1521 and claimed by Spain in 1667. Lujan was born on Guam. His parents were among the Spanish who colonized the Ladrones after 1667. Guam was the largest among the Ladrones, and the islands had become a key stop for the Spanish galleons—large trade ships capable of long voyages through rough weather—in their trade route from Spain to Acapulco and the Philippines. They were armed, and they left many a pirate ship listing on the high seas. They were also a hiding place for pirates that sailed the South China Sea. *Ladron* means "thief" in Spanish, so the islands became known as the Ladrones.

The piracy in the South China Sea in the nineteenth century was no different than that of the Somali of today. They countered the large Spanish galleons with small swift boats in which they could sidle up to a targeted vessel and make their demands. The Spanish sailors of that era were not genteel about their demands and expectations. In response, pirates were killed every day, and the galleons would pursue them, countering speed with heavy arms and long-range artillery. The captain and Lujan had many encounters, but they never lost a ship. They had been boarded more than once and won because of the fierce resistance of the crew. Lujan's linguistic skills made him a go-between when negotiations were required. He learned the skills for conflict resolution, skills which would stay with Lujan through his life.

Unfortunately, when it came time to clean up, Lujan was among the lower ranks that drew the duty. It was a smelly and sloppy process. The disemboweled remains were especially abhorrent; so was putting away the badly wounded. These aged Lujan prematurely and brought the dreams of horror his sleeping mind conjured.

Battling pirates was an adventure, but it also was a one-way trail to a short life. The many inlets and bays were prime places for sheltering pirates. To counter the threat, the Spanish brought in Spanish colonials in greater numbers to help rebalance the population of the Ladrones and marginalize the influence of the pirates. Pirates had shore lives like anyone else and were friends and relatives of many a Ladronian. Lujan played with their children before he went off to sea and relied on that camaraderie when attacking pirates were Ladronians. Along the way, he cruised the high seas for twenty years, encountering pirates as both friends and enemies.

By the time the sun rose on the morning that found the captain chatting with his cabin boy and tacking his ship into the Kona wind, it was 1865, and the American Civil War was over. European treaties were being signed by the Kingdom of Hawai'i, land was being carved up, and traditional lands were crumbling as the hooves of colonization marched on.

So this morning, Lujan told the captain of his desire to leave the ship at Ho'okena on the island of Hawai'i. During many stops at Ho'okena, Lujan had come to meet the local doctor, Dr. Trask, an Englishman who had built quite a practice, especially among the sailors and other English speakers of the area. He was in need of a houseboy to handle medical statements and records and provide general assistance to his growing practice. It was a good fit for Lujan's skills: he had sailed with the captain for nearly twenty years, had done the ship's record keeping, and at times had even helped with the captain's log. But Lujan and the captain could both see that world trade was emerging, fueling rapid growth in economies across the hemispheres. The economy of today was morphing into the economy of tomorrow right before their eyes. Tall ships were already turning little fishing wharves like Ho'okena into thriving international trade centers. All too soon would come the world traders, the sugar magnates, and the enterprising ranchers.

A new economics of craftsmanship was emerging. In addition to beef, herding of horses, horse breaking, slaughterhouses, meat processors, tanneries, and doctoring of cattle and people all kept the workforce innovative and healthy. Demand for new products grew in the form of wood posts and the newest wire for fencing and rope for lassoing on the ranches. Tools like Japanese sickles for weed work, cane knives with shorter and wider blades for slashing and cutting the cane (a design based on the Mexican machete), fertilizer, and other products were made specifically for the emerging sugar plantations along the coast north from Hilo to the Kohala and Kona uplands. On the windward side of Hawai'i, the aged lava flows had broken down into rich soil. Scottish and English traders planted the fertile loamy soil with sugarcane and another new economy was born.

Hawai'i's niche economy, while anchored in the sandalwood silk trade axis, was broadening that base into new fields; merchandise trading and transport, ship repair, fruit orchards, and fresh food and beef processing were turning places like Ho'okena into meccas of commerce.

The captain himself fancied the new products and economies, for they were making him a living. Like Lujan, he too left home to sail the seven seas. Now a captain, he lived well. He knew that Lujan's fate, like his, was tied to this economic tsunami. So the captain offered him his goodbyes and some British pounds so that Lujan would not have to ask for money to get started in Trask's employ. Lujan—the cabin boy, sailor of commerce, and pirate fighter—turned to face the wind, spun as if to cut the jib, and tacked his way up the plank and onto the warm sandy soil of Ho'okena.

Chapter Two

The Countryside

Kua'aina

The soft, warm sands caressed his sandaled feet, massaging them as he turned and walked away to head from the shore to the slopes of Ho'okena. His eyes met a myriad of paths and walkways. The paths were largely of dirt, and the walkways were paved with pebbles washed ashore by the relenting force of the Pacific tides. One pebbled walkway meandered toward a large house—a house he decided would likely be the Trask house. He drank in all the new colors, scents, and signature fragrances of the flowers and shrubs sprinkled along the way as he ambled up the path. It was a symphony of nature, and he broke out whistling a Spanish folk ditty called "Capotin": "Capo Capo tin tin tin tin esta noche vay illover, / Capo Capo tin tin tin tin manana amanecer. / No me mates con pistola, no me mates con punal, matame con tus boquitas y tus labias de coral." Roughly translated, it means "Tonight is going to rain, / Tomorrow will bring dawn. / So do not shoot me with your pistol, do not stab me with a dagger, but kill me with kisses from your coral lips." As he strolled up the path, he lulled into daydreaming about the melodic lyrics and the kisses of his *labias de coral*.

In the midst of his contrived concerto, he was struck by the myriad of colorful blossoms and shrubs that accentuated the pebbled paths. *Hau* (hibiscus) in many colors and the fragrances of other plants like the ever present *akulikuli* (ice plant or aloe vera) sprinkled among the sloping trails, anchoring themselves in the surrounding sandy soil.

Land in Hawai'i was divided into an ahupua'a, the basic land use unit. The ahupua'a was divided into sections beginning where the soil slipped into the sea from the upper plains and highlands of the mountain slopes. This seashore marked the first section of land. It was followed next by the loamy soil and plains good for farming and raising vegetable staples such as the '*uala* (sweet potato). The upper portion of the ahupua'a was the forest land—the source of wood for canoes, houses, and trade, especially the timber from the koa wood and sandalwood forests.

Ubiquitous in the Ho'okena lands were the kiawe trees supplying wood for cooking and charcoal and the *panini* (cactus), peppering the plains and growing in clumps under the most stark and difficult of conditions. Its fruit was prickly and its leaves edible. The *paniolos* called them *nopales* and ate the leaves with eggs and Portuguese milk bread, an island favorite import from the Portuguese. Both became pests from time to time as they spread their seed pods across the ahupua'a.

Cattle grazed freely on the upper grassy slopes held back in places by lava rock fences. Many were ornery and some were wild but both fell to the wiles and practices of the paniolo.

As Lujan turned his eyes back toward the house on the hill, he was pretty sure it was *Hale* (house) Trask. It was a plantation style house with a corrugated iron roof extending over a *lanai* (covered porch), twelve rooms including a parlor, combined kitchen/dining room, several bedrooms, and an office with an adjacent examining room. It was a far cry from the antiseptic environment of the English office and surgery of London. It was homey and inviting, welcoming patients and helping mute the fear some kanakas had about doctors.

The Hamakua Coast was next to North Kona and across from the Mauna Kea and Hualalai mountains. Cattle ranching was taking root in that area, especially the Parker Ranch founded by John Palmer Parker I. It was world-class in size. Ranching even spawned a new kanaka word: *paniolo*. It was a transliteration of the Spanish word *Hispaniolo* and was used to refer to the cowboys that came from Spanish-speaking countries, especially Mexico. These paniolo called themselves *vaqueros*, Spanish for "cowboys." Both terms were used in Hawai'i.

Raising cattle fit in nicely with the climate and soil. Grass grew bountifully. Parker Ranch became the world's largest ranch owned by one person. Parker imported horses, cattle, and leather goods; and tanning, slaughter, and other cattle-based enterprises bloomed. Saddle making and ornamentation required craftsmanship that was easily learned and quickly became an art form. Local hardwoods like kiawe, koa, and *kuawa* (guava) were used for the base skeletal structure of the saddle and the saddle tree. The skeletal saddle was then hand crafted with leather and woven to fit an individual cowboy's torso.

Local talent blending with imported technique led to new products and handicrafts, further kindling growth in the villages around Ho'okena. This was a good place to be, and Lujan could feel it in the bones of his daydreaming soul.

Chapter Three

The Family

Ke 'Ohana

Lujan knocked at the rear entry to the Trask house. There was no clear upstairs/downstairs culture of the sort found in the spacious doctors' houses of London. He had seen those. But for tiny Ho'okena, this was a house of substance. It was big by local standards. People came to the doctor to be treated, and Trask also made home visits as time permitted. He had a small infirmary in the back of the house and a waiting room on the side. Toward the front was a parlor and a dining room. What mattered to the locals was less the building itself than the fact that healing took place behind its walls. If there was healing, there probably also were miracles. And that brought Trask respect and legitimacy.

Trask also took to working with the local *kahuna*, professionals in many fields—among them medical doctors. They often sat and conversed over their practices. Trask would sometimes prescribe a Hawaiian herbal medicine. The kahuna liked that. Then of course, there was the harbor. Western medicines could be ordered from Honolulu or elsewhere. This kept Trask quite satisfied with his tiny little practice in this tiny little town.

Lujan unpacked his modest clothes and tools, including his favorite slide rule. He still had a love/hate relationship with it. But when he thought of these things, he realized that already new technologies of the day were making new demands on his skills. For example, Trask's accounts were in some disarray, evidence that the new economy and demand for services were growing faster than Trask's ability to make a record of them. In addition, there were no clear rules about equivalency for bartering. Lujan figured he had better start there, for a quick look suggested that balanced ledgers were the first step to building a profit. He also needed to put in place a consistent billing schedule. He needed to follow up on bills. He had to calculate a pricing structure, initiate a credit system, and deal with individual payment plans.

Accounts aside, all work and no play left the doctor fatigued and plain grumpy. Lujan, the doctor's assistant, also needed time away from his little desk. He took to having conversations with the house maid Kaililau—at least that was the name locals gave the kanaka maid who lived and worked in Trask's house. He realized that he was eighteen years older than she was, and he took care not to take advantage of that.

Yet he was smitten by her beauty and her fascinating name, Kaililau. All kanaka names—*inoa*—have meanings. Family lore and ancient land records—*palapala sila nui*—have it that her full name was Elizabeth Kaililau Kaale (Palea). In our ʻohana, *ili* means "land" and "inheritance," and *lau* means "leaf" or "cover." Together these translate into the source who protects and strengthens the ʻohana and through whom the inheritance passes. *Lau* also means "many," and she was to have thirteen children; as the Lujan 'ohana grew, all of its land would flow through her.

In kanaka lore, there often is a legend attached to an inoa. There is a legend about Kaililau. It is entitled The Covering of the Koa Leaf. *Kaili* means "skin" or "covering"; *lau* is "leaf"; *o* is "of"; and *koa* is the koa tree. The legend of Kaililau presented here is the translated version of William Hyde Rice in *Hawaiian Legends*, 1977.

"Kaililauokekoa was the only daughter of Moikeha and Ho'oipo, two very high chiefs of Kaua'i. Her parents loved the child greatly and gave her every care, engaging a nurse or *kahu* to be with her always. As Kaililauokekoa grew, her beauty increased. After she had ridden the surf at Makaiwa near Waipouli, or had played konane—a complicated game resembling chess—her cheeks glowed like the rising sun.

"One day, when her parents had gone to cultivate taro in Kapahi, Kaililauokekoa was alone playing konane with her nurse. Suddenly a strange man stood before the door. He asked the girl if she enjoyed konane very much. When she answered that she did, he suggested that she play a game with him. Kaililauokekoa won the game by a score of nine to four. She said to the stranger, 'You have been defeated by the daughter of Moikeha.'

"The man asked, 'Is Moikeha still living?'

"'Yes,' answered Kaililauokekoa. 'He has gone to the taro patches now. Moikeha loves surf riding and my mother. He will stay on Kaua'i till he dies.'

"After the stranger had heard these words, he said, 'I believed that he was dead. I regret not being able to take him back to Molokai with me. When he returns, tell him that the high chief of Molokai has been here and been defeated by Moikeha's daughter in a game. Give your father and mother the *aloha* of Heaa-kekoa.'

"When the chief from Molokai had spoken these words, he got into his canoe and started for his island.

"Now, at Pihanakalani, where all good things abounded—a legendary spot on Kaua'i above the Wailua River that cannot be found nowadays—there lived two very high chiefs; Kauakahialii, The Battle of the Lone Chief; and sister, Kahalelehua, The House of Lehua. In this garden spot of Pihanakalani was the far famed fountain of Waiokeola, Water of Life, which could restore the dead to life and renew the youth of the aged. Kauakahialii owned a very loud-sounding flute called Kanikawi, which could be heard as far away as Kapaa.

"One night, Kaililauokekoa had been playing konane with her nurse until midnight. That night, while the girl slept, the nurse heard the flute crying, 'Kaililauokekoa, do you sleep?'

"When the girl awoke in the morning, her nurse told her the words she had heard. Kaililauokekoa was greatly excited, and she said, 'Today we shall sleep all day so that I may be awake at midnight, for I must hear his voice from the hills when it calls me.'

"So they slept until evening. Then they played konane to keep themselves awake. At midnight, they heard the flute voice calling, 'Kaililauokekoa, do you sleep in Puna? Is not the surf high?'

"'I do not sleep. I shall search for you until I find you,' answered the breathless *Kaililauokekoa*.

"Then she and her nurse started on their search. They climbed up the mountainside and at daylight reached *Kuamoo*.

"When the sister of the flute player saw these two women coming she sent heavy mist and the blinding rain to delay their journey. They found shelter in a hollow tree and when the rain had ceased they went on. *Kaililauokekoa*, soon saw a house where a bright fire was burning.

As the two women approached the house of *Ka-hale-lehua*, the sister of the flute player, she took pity on them and welcomed them. She took off their wet clothes and gave them each a dry *pa'u* (women's skirt). Then she prepared a meal for her unbidden guests. She placed before them a platter of *lipoa limu*, choice seaweed, and little striped *manini* fish, still alive. *Kaililauokekoa* was greatly surprised to see the live fish, and said to her nurse, 'We live near the sea yet we never have live fish. This place is far from the sea. How is it that the fish are still alive?'

"Her hostess answered her by saying that she and her brother had a fishpond near their house.

"After the meal was finished, Kaililauokekoa went in search of the flute that had called her away from home. She came to the room of Kauakahialii and found the flute hidden in his breast. At once, a great love for this chief filled the heart of the girl, and she forgot her fond parents and stayed with him.

"When the parents of Kaililauokekoa found that their daughter was gone, they began to search for her. At last they came to the house where she was living with the young chief and carried them both to Kapaa. There they tied the chief to a post in a house.

"The first day, he was given nothing to eat. On the second day, a boy passed by and seeing the prisoner, asked if he had been given any food or water. When he heard that he had received none, he returned to his parents and made known to them the chief's condition. They ordered their son to put water in a coconut shell and to get another one for food so that he could throw them to the prisoner. With these he crawled through the rushes so that no one would see him.

"The boy carried out his parents' instructions on that day and many following days. The chief began to look well again.

"When the father of Kaililauokekoa had recovered from his anger, he called his daughter to him and asked her to explain to him how she came to be in the mountains. She told him that she had heard the flute calling to her and had wanted to make of the man who played it either a husband or a friend.

"Her parents decided to allow the kahunas to settle the matter. When they were called together and had heard the story, they all agreed that Kaililauokekoa should marry the chief if he could give his genealogy. As soon as Kauakahialii was called before them, he proved that he was a very high chief, and so the beautiful chiefess was given to him in marriage. The boy who had carried food and water to the chief in prison became his great friend and was made *luna*, or head man, over all his lands."

And this is how the story ends.

Here you have two women—one a legend, the other a living person. They pursue love each in their own way. And they share the same name. Their root name is Kaililau, which can translate to mean a covering or protective leaf. The legendary one is defined as the covering leaf of the koa. The other name is taken to mean covering or protecting the inheritance, the *kuleana* land, of the family 'ohana. She bore thirteen children; and with her husband, Lucas, she patched together 210 acres during her lifetime. Through her children, especially Samuel Ho'olohekamohoali'i, she protected the *kuleana*, the land thrived, and the 'ohana grew in unbroken lineage to the present.

Legend aside and back at Trask's clinic, Lujan the bookkeeper took to extending the chats he and Kaililau had with walks through the lava fields of *'a'a* (sliding lava) and *pahoehoe* (gliding lava). He spun enticing yarns and told the tales of his worldwide voyages and visits. He recounted stories of pirates and how he and the captain had fought off the devils in hand-to-hand combat. He spoke of how they fought raging fires on the wooden decks. Kaililau was taken by the romance and mystery of it all. She was—as the *kanaka* say—*ho'ohia'ai*, enchanted by the spell he wove. He in turn found her exotic, with her fair brown complexion and her stories of life in her 'aina and her training to become a maid for Trask. Kaililau relished helping in the infirmary, especially treating the elders and hearing their tales of times past.

She learned about palpating the body, the herbs Trask used with his patients, and the idea of treating the whole body as practiced by the kahuna. Trask specifically used herbal teas to treat diabetes, a killer of kanakas. Kaililau visited Lujan as often as she could, taking care when they met to wear one of the nice dresses Trask had bought for her on her birthdays. She quickly succumbed to the keeper of books and slayer of pirates.

Lujan was especially taken by her stories of the paniolo living on the ranches between Kona and Kukai'au on the Hamakua Coast. The cattle were fattened on the plump native grasses of the region. The paniolo then drove them to wharves like Ho'okena that dotted the coastline, especially from Mahukona, near Kohala; to Kawaihae, with its deep harbor; and on past Kona and Miloli'i to Kaalualu and Honoapo in Ka'u. Upon arrival at one of these wharves, the *pipi* (cattle) were driven into the water and made to swim to the ship where they were loaded on board. It was a time full of whistles, coaxing with a click of the tongue and the fetching call to come—"*Hele mai.*" The *pipi nuha* (stubborn) cattle were roped, cajoled, and lassoed onto the deck, the worse for wear and frothing for air.

And so it was that smiles grew to chats in the stairwells, holding of hands during walks, handwritten notes passed on by others in the house, storytelling, and then intimacy. It was hard to keep from spilling the poi in such a small house. Knowing this and the good reputation he had built with Trask, they were discreet.

They soon married with Trask's permission. The ceremony and the hymns—the *himeni*—were spoken in kanaka maoli. Trask had few parties like this one. Both the bride and groom were alumni of the doctor's kindness and generosity, and Trask would miss them both. He worried that the child bride was thirteen, and Lujan was thirty-two. He prayed that they would share a long and loving life.

Lujan began looking around for a place to live since they were ready for a family. Soon Kaililau was more than ready; she was with child (*hapai*).

Through Trask's patients and some of the paniolo whom Lujan had befriended over the years, Lujan heard of a seven-acre lot available in Waiki'i, nestled in the foothills above the Parker Ranch.

Elizabeth Kaale Palea born in 1860 at Peleau, Hawaii.
Samuel's mother.

Lucas Puanani Lujan born in 1845 in Guam.
Samuel's father.

Kaililau packed up her few belongings. Lujan gathered his remnants of nearly twenty years at sea as well as his expanded wardrobe, records, and books. He was now a professional and respected accountant and occasional paniolo. And he was, after all, an *espaniolo*. He was in fact a swarthy solid man, five and one half feet tall with bronzed skin and a bold mustache. He spoke several languages, was an admired conversationalist, and his voice was mellow; it drew attention in a crowd or in intimate soliloquy and every day chats. Most notably, he had a way with women.

In a short time, he was to become a farmer of seven acres, toiling in the cool breezes that rolled from the Kawaihae wharf up the loamy slopes of the twin towns of Waimea and Kamuela (named after Samuel Parker). Kamuela came to be after annexation via the United States Post Office which needed a name other than Waimea, already a town on Kaua'i. Used to the warmth in Kona, Kaililau was less comfortable in the cold Waiki'i winds, so her pregnancy was not always the joy she had envisioned. Lujan raised vegetables, or more likely, the vegetables raised him. Kaililau gave birth to Emelia in 1876, the centennial of the American Declaration of Independence. But there was no room for that sort of big-world culture in little Waiki'i. There, for the lovers from Ho'okena, Emelia was the whole wide world.

The seven-acre plot in Waiki'i was a part of the larger economic change taking place in Hawai'i. In 1848, Kamehameha III (Kauikeaouli) decreed the Great Mahele, or land division. At the time, the land was divided into three types: the *moku* (a district of land), the ahupua'a (a land division stretching from the uplands to the sea), and the *ili* (a subdivision). In an effort to help kanakas reconnect with '*aina* (the land), Kamehameha divided the of ahupua'a land into three parts: the royal lands for the king (*moi'*), smaller parcels for the chiefs (*ali'i nui*) and district chiefs (*ali'i moku*), and in small lots for the commoners (*maka'ainana*).

The birth right for commoners translated into seven acres or less for a blood kanaka. Kaililau had family on the Hamakua Coast in North Hilo. Before the Great Mahele, their land was an ahupua'a—a division of land running from the mountain edge to a sloping midsection with lush soil and then to the water's edge at the ocean. The side boundaries were identified by measuring the distance from the middle of the nearest stream or gulch on each side of the land strip. In those days, kanakas did not use the western compass.

In North Hilo, the directions were *mauka* (inland to the forest edge where trees grew) and *makai* (by the water where fishing thrived), and then on each local area or landmark known among kanakas. On the island of Hawai'i, these *moku* were Hilo, the largest town (south) and Hamakua, the largest land area with its lush valleys and loamy soil (north). The family 'aina stretched from *mauka* (the edge of the forest of Mauna Kea) to *makai* (the rough sea cliffs of the ocean) then north to the middle point of Opea Stream and south toward Hilo to the middle of 'Awapuhi Stream. This area was known as Opea Peleau. The family was fairly large, so all seven acre allotments put together amassed over a hundred acres. It was a promising sum, but one had to be realistic because already there was talk about kanakas selling their land for a pittance or some *'okolehao* (liquor), although the extent to which this actually happened had been exaggerated. Like all exaggerations, it bent the truth and overstated the issue.

In any event, Lujan felt that with Kaililau carrying her first child, she needed a place with more room. So he packed the modest belongings he shared with Kaililau and set off in a horse and buggy wagon for Peleau. There were two crosscutting routes to Peleau. One was from Waik'i'i over the edge of Mauna Kea, down to Kaumana, and thence north to Ha'aheo on the north tip of Hilo. Then it would go over the Hamakua coastal trail through Onomea, Pepe'ekeo, then Hakalau, and on to Kauniho and Lepoloa Homesteads. Thence it would be half a mile to Opea Peleau Village.

The trail would wind all along the way through the streams and gulches and the sugar plantations he had heard about. He also heard that it rained every day on that route. Kaililau was ready to birth, so this might not be the wisest route to take.

The other route was to take the trail from *Waiki'i* to Kamuela and Waimea down through the Parker Ranch toward Honoka'a. It passed by the large impassable valley of Waipio to Ahualoa and the Hamakua trail to dry Pa'auhau. The trail then meandered on to the rocky shores of Laupahoehoe, past Honohina to Opea Gulch, and up a small rise to Peleau.

Lujan chose the route via the Parker Ranch for what he gauged was a three-day trip. It took four and the generosity of a paniolo from the Kukai'au Ranch.

Lujan's horse had pulled a shoe on the lava rock along the trail in Pa'auhau. The horse would not last long without good shoes to buttress its pounding hooves against the sharp pahoehoe lava that was coming next on the trail at Laupahoehoe. Kaililau laughed heartily at the play with words here. Her name, Kaililau, meant "leaf," as did the *lau* in *Laupahoehoe*. *Lau* also meant "to protect." The play was that the horse needed a covering or protection (the horse shoe) against the sharp edged pahoehoe lava. With the help of a Portuguese cowboy from the Ramos Ranch, Lujan shoed the horse and set off for Peleau.

Upon reaching Peleau, Lujan settled in to find himself a job and a home for Kaililau and little Emelia. There was a one-room house for her uncle Samuel Hoolohe to use. He was Kaililau's *makua kane* (uncle) and would later name her son Samuel Ho'olohekamohoali'i

Lucas Lujan after *makua kane* Samuel Ho'olohe. The newcomers were welcomed, and they settled into the small tack house where the saddles were hung. It was not that large, but it was private, a luxury with the baby. But most of all, Kaililau was happy that Peleau was warm like Kona. It was a good time for the 'ohana as she was birthing. Emelia was the first, born in 1876. Then came Mary (1878), George (1879), Lizzie (1882), Annie (1884), Sussanah (1887), George K. (1889), Lillie (1891), Samuel Ho'olohekamohoali'i Lucas Lujan (1894), Lucas P. Lujan (1896), Keahiulaokalani (1899), Christina (1900), and Lizzie (1903).

Samuel Lujan family photo taken at the original Lujan family house in Peleau. Samuel is in the front row on the right in a double breasted coat.

While Kaililau was having and raising thirteen children, Lucas took his accounting and other skills to the Honohina Sugar Plantation. The sugarcane business was growing so rapidly that immigrants had to be brought in. Folks like Lujan were driving Hawaii's economy with their skills. Knowing this, Lujan made a vow to the family that they were all going to go to school. They were to get the skills needed to succeed in the midst of this boom. To that end, Lujan bought four of the older horses being put to pasture by the plantation. The family would use these four horses to get to school. They were to attend by age. When one completed school, the vacant saddle would go to the next one in the queue for school. This was education on the installment plan. It worked.

The plantation manager was a gruff Scot of short stature. He was all business. He took to Lujan, who was all work. The accounting skills and tricks in animal husbandry he had picked up from the Kamuela paniolo made him attractive to Ross, the Scotsman. Lujan was hired as stable master on the spot, and his new life began.

The stable had several hundred horses and mules. The mules were used to take the cut cane, wrapped in bundles by the cutters, to the wooden flumes carrying water from the many nearby gulches. The cutters armed with cane knives harvested the cane by using broad-bladed knives with a sharp hook at the upper corner. By snagging the cane stalk with that hook and then grabbing the stalk with the free hand, cutters could cut the stalks in required sizes for transport to the sugar mills. The process was driven by a network of flumes. Main flumes were large and stationary. Narrower feeder flumes were taken from field to field when harvesting was underway. This was the latest practice in harvesting cane, and Lujan absorbed it all. He redesigned the carrying frames used for holding bundles on the mules. To keep the horses and mules less prone to injury, he built stronger bundle frames and rimmed the uneven bundle ends.

For nutrition, he took the throwaway molasses of the milling process, mixed it with green Napier grass, a corn-like plant full of nutrition, and served it to the animals each day. Scrawny mules were no longer a thing in the herds. Lujan was to spend a career overseeing the Honohina stables and assuring their health and energy. With innovations like these, he was a man before his time. The overseers and *lunas* (field supervisors) were especially pleased with the horses they used. Day by day, Lujan's influence with management grew and the respect of the field hands as well. And day by day one more, Lujan was on the way to school, leaving no vacant saddles or empty desks behind.

As the Lujan 'aina was growing on the land of Hawai'i, another family was in the making. Two young Portuguese from the Madeira Islands were about to start their *familia Portugues*. She was thirteen and from Madeira Island in the Azores, and he was about nine years her elder and from San Miguel. They were on a trading vessel hauling merchandise from Lisbon and families from the Azores headed to Hawai'i. Augusta Cambra and Amos Joaquin Ignacio had come as part of a group of Portuguese families signing on as contract labor in the kanaka sugar plantations. In Amos Joaquin Ignacio's case, he was coming as a contract school teacher. You see, when the Scotch immigrants came, they brought the Portuguese as the first immigrant labor force. The Portuguese had a long record of sugar agriculture in the Azores. The Scotch had tried on Kaua'i to use kanakas as labor. But the Scotch were go-by-the-book managers. So there was no room for the flexibility kanakas preferred. The old timers, kama'aina, say that in Miloli'i near Kona—when the fish began to run the kanakas stopped work, grabbed their nets, and went off to fish—this clash of style would persist. Many would learn that centuries of culture-wide values and behaviors would not be overcome by imported laborers, English language classes, and religion.

Soon there was to be a Jacob's Ladder afoot as the tiers of skill and education emerged differentiated by culture. The Portuguese quickly became the experienced hands, and they rose to management support positions. So another cheaper replacement labor source was found. After the Portuguese, the Chinese, Japanese, Puerto Rican, and Filipino workers came in that order. The last of these sailed into Hilo in 1948 with a shipload of young Filipinos, mostly Ilocano speakers, plus a few Visayan speakers, all headed for the plantation camps.

Meanwhile the Portuguese ship rounded the cape and headed for Hawai'i. The voyage was rough, and several of the children died. There was also the worry of infections, the flu, and the so-called sailor's sickness, scurvy. Scurvy is a Vitamin C deficiency treated by keeping limes in the sailor's diet. Hence came the term *limey* as the nickname for English sailors.

None of these diseases would keep the strong-willed Augusta down. Pestilence paled as her romance with Amos Joaquin bloomed. Amos Joaquin asked for Augusta's hand in marriage from Sr. Cambra and had received it. Cambra felt that marriage to a school teacher meant a sound job to support a Portuguese family. In the Hawai'i of that time, a large Portuguese family was to be celebrated—the more working hands there were, the better the family's economic status. With consent in hand and the winds of romance in the air, it seemed to Augusta that marriage to Amos Joaquin was a crowning gift for her on her thirteenth birthday. She was elated.

As the slopes of Mauna Kea and Mauna Loa rose on the horizon, the steam ship SS Kinau moved swiftly toward the landing at Honoipo. Honoipo is on the Kohala shore of the Alanuihaha Channel between Maui and Kohala. The Portuguese on board were contracted labor with the Kohala plantation in Hawi. The Alanuihaha is the roughest channel in Hawaii's oceans. So soon enough, the less resistant were leaning over the side, heaving and praying to leave the ship for the warm rocks and wind-sculpted sands of Honoipo.

Honoipo was a desolate, rocky, windblown, cactus-sprouting place of necessity. It was close to Kohala Sugar Company and the Wight family's ranch horse pastures. The deep water wharf could accommodate both ventures. The sugar company had some temporary homes for newcomers. These were little three- and four-room bungalows. Augusta Cambra and Amos Joaquin Ignacio married. Because the school house was in Hawi Village, and the Kohala plantation headquarters were there, the Ignacios had priority in housing. So they moved to Hawi. The family came shortly thereafter as Augusta was with child.

On a sunny Kohala day, Alice Pauline Ignacio was born to 13 year old Augusta. She was the first of 10 children. It was 1903 in *Hawai'i*. Baby Alice was bright, healthy and grew fast. By age five, her father, the school teacher principal of a one room school house was already teaching her English and introducing her to the skills of reading. Like Lujan on the other side of the island, education was going to be the pathway to the future, one horse at a time in *Peleau* and one child at a time in Hawi.

As the Ignacios grew in number, so did the school house. After Alice, there were Antonina, Edith, Amos Andrew, Norman, Albert, Mabel, Laura, Clarence, and Elsa. There were six girls and four boys. Five, including Alice, became school teachers.

After several years, Amos Joaquin had the opportunity to move as principal to a larger school at O'okala on the Hamakua Coast. He held this principal-ship for quite a few years and moved his family to Waipunalei Village. He ended his career at John M. Ross School in Ninole, also on the Hamakua Coast. By now, his daughter Alice and several grandchildren were going to "Grandpa's school" in Ninole, where Alice was the sixth grade teacher. Antonina was the next in age and served as principal at Pepe'ekeo, then at Hilo Union, and finally at the Keakealani School in Volcano. Edith was next and was a principal in Honolulu. And finally there was Norman, the agriculture teacher at Baldwin High School on Maui. The Ignacio family was leaving its mark on education in *Hawai'i*. That said, it was time for the house of Lujan and the house of Ignacio to ally.

Chapter Four

The Uncommon Alliance

Ka Hui Laha'ole

The Lujan uncommon alliance—*ka hui laha'ole*—began when Alice Pauline Ignacio was sixteen. The Ignacios had moved by now from O'okala to Umauma so that Amos Joaquin Ignacio could become principal at John M. Ross School in Ninole. Housing was limited there, and most of the family was still at home. Ten children doubled and tripled was just not going to work. So Augusta and Amos Joaquin scoured the villages between Ninole and the Portuguese plantation at Wailea, located on the way to Hilo. The Ignacios learned of a house at Umauma next to Peleau. They took it and began to settle in. The house was a short walk of ten minutes to the train stop of the Hilo Railroad Company (later the Hilo Consolidated Railroad) at Peleau. The trail to the station was on Lujan's property and Lujan had given the railroad an easement for the railroad to use that strip of land. The Isa, Nonaka, Arita, Ignacio, Ka'aua, Takazaki families and the

Chinese *(pake)* plantation camp workers all used the trail. They were pleased about Lujan's generosity over the easement.

Partnerships and alliances can come together in strange ways. In the Spain that Lujan knew as a child, families were tight social organizations that influenced and often controlled land, family relations, prosperity, and war. In Hawai'i, the 'ohana was also a society where families underpinned all aspects of social, economic, religious, and political life. It had helped Lujan find a place to raise a family. What is more, Kaililau's culture was inclusive; Lujan the Spaniard was welcomed, and he learned the Hawaiian language and customs. The two cultures coexisted, and this enriched both cultures. Lujan's multilingual and technological skills were especially important in light of the rapid economic growth of the day. The culture of Spain transplanted to the Ladrones was more colonial and marginalized the native Chamorro culture of the Ladrones. An inclusive culture and an educated family would make the 'ohana respected, and he intended to make this the guiding light in raising the Lujan family.

So when the railroad easement issue came up, Lujan did the generous thing by allowing it. At Peleau alone, Japanese, kanaka, Portuguese, Filipino, and Chinese would board and join riders from all the multicultures on the Hamakua Coast. The Ignacio girls brought new life to the little village on 'Awapuhi Stream. The train rides were a seed bed for growing the next generation of acquaintances, relationships, and leaders. It also helped spawn the uncommon alliance between a hybrid Spanish kanaka 'ohana and a Portuguese family. This melding was eased by the shared Iberian culture, religion, and the proximate languages of Spain and Portugal. This melding was most evident in religion. The Lujan kanakas became Catholics. Multicultural students on the long ride from

Honoka'a to Hilo whiled the time away with pleasantries, sharing stories of their cultures and the chitchat that rolling wheels spawn.

The Spanish culture honed by interactions with the native Chamorros of Guam gave him linguistic tools others would not have. The shared culture with the Portuguese was especially helpful both socially and religiously for Lujan. With language not posing a problem, new interactions and friendships could be built, making it easier to penetrate the layers of cultural barriers which guard the culture in the continuum from formal and group to informal and personal.

This worked for Lujan with one notable exception—the Ignacio family and its female patriarch, Augusta Cambra Ignacio. She and Lujan clashed. She thought him to be arrogant, crude, and lesser bred. He considered her prickly, prone to pout, and controlling to the extreme. He was always polite to her, but he kept his distance. The relationship came to loggerheads when the wings of gossip and rumor took to the air over the relationship between Samuel Ho'olohekamohoali'i and Alice Pauline Ignacio. As word of her disapproval took flight, Lujan became much more open about his stance. He let it be known that he was not opposed to the possibility of union between the families. This was too tempting for Augusta to let pass by, so she turned to her weapon of choice—the silent treatment. He parried with an overabundance of politeness.

There was one layer of relationships which Lujan never let penetrate. It was the nature of his family in Guam. In family chats and discussions of family, Lujan added nothing and was adept at changing the subject before it got too close to the delicate topic. Lujan did have siblings but shared little about them. It is worth remembering that Lujan left home at age nine. And he lived much longer on ships than he did on land in a family setting. As a result, his home in Peleau became his permanent home; his family there was his 'ohana.

Samuel Ho'olohekamohoali'i Lucas Lujan was the ninth of Lucas Lujan's thirteen children. His Christian name was Samuel. His kanaka name is one with a variety of meanings. *Lohe*, "to listen," is the root word. *Moho* is "to carry out." *Ali'i* is "a leader." *Ho'olohe* means "to hear" and "obey or carry out." *Kamohoali'i* means "having the ear of the chief."

According to Pukui and Elbert (1965), Kamohoali'i was a ranking chief and was Pele's older and favorite brother who was the most celebrated of the ancestral shark gods; he was also the one who accompanied Pele from *Kahiko* (ancestral land) to Hawai'i. He had a human form as well as shark (*hilu*) fish forms. He was also Pele's royal selected one. The 'ohana blended these ideas into "the royal selected one who has the ear of the chief, listens, carries out, and leads." This inoa was especially apt for the 'ohana as the shark is the family *'aumakua* (totem). Over the years, as he consolidated the 'ohana 'aina, Samuel Ho'olohekamohoali'i would become the family leader—its kupuna.

Samuel Ho'olohekamohoali'i Lucas Lujan met the Ignacios and was especially taken by the older sisters, particularly Alice. Alice was a beauty. She had long wavy black hair and a figure to knock you out. She had a beauty spot on her left cheek that was eye catching. She was amused by "Sammy," as she liked to call him. Remember too that his pathway to adulthood was not typical. Samuel Ho'olohekamohoali'i was born in 1894 and she in 1903. He was nine years her senior. But then he remembered his father and mother and the difference in their ages. It was eighteen years.

He worried more about his relationship in school. He did not start school until the vacant saddle was open to him. He was twelve when he went to elementary school. He had gone to Hilo Boarding School for kanakas and did well as a student. He even learned how to pump the school organ there. He met friends who had connections, and being more mature than most, he got exposed to the social issues of his generation. And he met the sons of chiefs. His favorite connection was with the son of the king of Tonga. He and the Tongan ali'i became close friends. Samuel Ho'olohekamohoali'i had him to the house on holidays or weekends. For the Tongan, *poi* (the starch staple of the Polynesian diet), *opelu* (salted mackeral), *laulau* (steamed pork), beef, butterfish wrapped in young taro leaf, and *kulolo* (a coconut and taro pudding) were candy to his Polynesian palate.

After boarding school, Samuel Ho'olohekamohoali'i went to Honolulu to stay with his *makuahine hanauna* (aunty) Rose Farm and attend McKinley High School, where he came to love the sciences, especially chemistry. His first job was at the local sugar mill as the sampler of the sugar curing process of the harvested cane. Samples were taken all along the curing process as the sugar heated. These samples guided the cooking process to assure quality. It led him to take chemistry to enhance his knowledge and his chances to work full time at the local sugar mill.

Then there was Alice, the schoolteacher-to-be. She had her own goals. She was sixteen when she graduated from high school. She wanted to go to normal school and become a teacher. But her eye was on Samuel Ho'olohekamohoal'i who was nine years her senior. She was sixteen when their dalliance turned into serious courtship. He was twenty-five. He was already working at the sugar mill, so he had a job. Then there were all those other Portuguese and Chinese girls on the train who flattered Samuel Ho'olohekamohoali'i. The pressure grew as did her dilemma. It was either post–high school (normal school) study to become a teacher or wedlock and having babies. And Samuel Ho'olohekamohoali'i had his dilemma: more school to pursue chemistry or stay as the plantation sugar sampler.

The dilemmas boiled down to this. Alice started school one year early because she was born in the school year (January 1903). She was six. The year was 1909. She graduated at age sixteen. Samuel Ho'ohekamohoali'i started school at age twelve on the vacant saddle. He went to Hilo Boarding School then to high school. He proposed to Alice when she was sixteen. She said no. She knew her mother Augusta would refuse, and she wanted to be a teacher anyway.

Alice was born to be a pacesetter. She started school a year early. She went to normal school and made her "Sammy" wait as she got the building blocks of her career put in place. She built Samuel Ho'olohekamohoali'i's support and respect for her career ladder. She would get a college degree and beget children in a balance that few women of the era displayed. While the amendment to the US constitution allowing women to vote was just being looked at, Alice was off to the educational race she needed, so her dreams could come true.

Meanwhile, Samuel Ho'olohe'kamohoali'i graduated from McKinley High School in Honolulu on June 21, 1917, and did so with honors. Alice had just graduated from Hilo High School on June 23, 1922. He was twenty-three years old and working. She had hoped that he might let her go to normal school for her teaching credential. Samuel Ho'olohekamohoali'i was already working at Hakalau plantation and doing well. And he wanted to study chemistry. So what to do? That was the obvious dilemma. Should a man let his love have a career and have that career go first? Should a woman let her love go first? The latter was tradition. The former was change and more equal treatment for women. This was 1923; as noted above, although women could vote, they were still second in most everything else.

Not for Alice. She and Samuel Ho'olohekamohoali'i talked things through as they always did. He cared deeply about chemistry. Perhaps there was a compromise that Alice would accept. For Samuel Ho'olohekamohoali'i, it was her love and the depth of his personal feelings about her that mattered. Samuel Ho'olohekamohoali'i had indeed first proposed to Alice at age sixteen. But her mother would be opposed even though Augusta was only thirteen when she married Amos Joaquin and had Alice. No matter what, Augusta would not approve of Samuel H'olohekamohoali'i because he was *hapa* (half) kanaka and because she wanted Alice to marry a Portuguese.

Until Alice was twenty-one, Augusta had been the thorn that pricked at will. This made Alice's life intolerable. It was now 1923 when she was turning twenty-one, and Samuel Ho'olohekamohoali'i had finished high school and had a job at the plantation mill. And he also still had his ambition for studying science. Their affection for each other helped make life livable, but they knew that things had to change sooner rather than later. After three years of talking and waiting, Alice was finally twenty-one. Augusta could no longer rule Alice's life. So in the midst of the Christmas holidays, Samuel Ho'olohekamohoali'i proposed again. She agreed to marry him if he let her go to normal school. He agreed and during December 19, 1924, Alice and her "Sammy" married.

As their love was unusual, so was their wedding. Her "Sammy" picked her up from her teaching job at O'okala School on Friday at 2:00 p.m., and they simply eloped. She told her father, Amos Joaquin, what she was doing, and Amos quietly gave his blessing. They were married by Father Gabriel Feron with no one from the family present. The rest was a "Sammy" surprise. Sammy took her for a ride from O'okala to Waimea and then toward Kawaihae down the highway toward the beach, retracing the steps of the path that Lucas and Kaililau had taken on that fateful ride from Waiki to Peleau.

He turned off the main highway at the next trail and drove to a roadside flat spot and parked. On the barren rock studded with cactus, they camped under the stars. As if that were not enough, he took her hunting, and they shot the pheasant for their nuptial dinner. They went to bed to a symphony of crickets under the stars.

Chapter Five

The Blight

Ke Eleao

From the Great Mahele in 1848 to the forced annexation of Hawai'i to the United States in 1898, kanakas lived through years of blight. *Eleao* means "blight" in Hawaiian, and more particularly, it refers to the blight of insects that attack the leaf of the sugarcane. Looking at it as a kanaka might is looking at it in this way: growth and profit for the planters and other economic moguls, but years of decline in the land grant culture and heart of the kanakas. Even in the Great Mahele, foreigners received many more land grants than the commoners (*maka'ainana*), farmers, and others of that economic level because foreigners understood land ownership—a foreign concept to kanakas. The sugar industry was the great spawner of competition over the land. While they profited, the commoners lost their land as many kanakas had no sense of its long term value; they sold at prices that were sheer robbery and often included high interest rates on loans. Ranchers differed. While their desire for land was voracious, at least they used the grants to give jobs to the kanaka paniolo. In most places, the veneer of activities to "help" kanakas and their land was a mask over the economic reality of monopolies and the rapid increase in the moguls of wealth. At least, this was the view of many of the kanakas.

The sugar plantations brought many new ways and practices to Hawai'i, beginning with the importation of immigrants to work the cane fields. In that regard, Hawai'i looked more like the slavery driven south in the United States than Hawai'i after the cane knife. From 1848 and the Great Mahele to 1898 and the annexation of Hawai'i, kanakas would shrink in gross numbers yet increase in the number among those left in poverty. And the irony was that the *haole* (non-kanaka), who came initially to convert and civilize, took and destroyed the culture and left in its wake a blight on Hawaii's economy, culture, and language.

The era from the Mahele to annexation was a period of profound change resulting from the failed effort among kanakas to adapt to the new ways and more importantly, to find paths to bend and sculpt these ways to fit better the kanaka way. Mixing and blending were the obvious tools. So the Lujan alliance and the Ignacio focus on education was "spot on," as they would say in England. The two-room schools all around Hawai'i were places where literacy would become a tool for letting youth do more than just learn the language of the colonizer. But to enable the youth to understand the imposing culture and to find ways to mitigate its influence on the youth—that was the challenge. This was why Sammy's willingness to let Alice go to normal school was so powerful and symbolic. How many would do that in the 1920s? How many would wait for the vacant saddle and start school with students nearly a decade their juniors? Lucas Lujan had the foresight and courage to make education the guiding light for his journey through life and a major crossover from the Lucas Luján 'ohana to the Samuel Ho'olohekamohoali'i 'ohana. Sam Luján, as most people called him, was not just a dreamer of dreams. He lived them. He had a bedrock sense of politics and people who kept those dreams in the realm of the pragmatic, and he had a wife who kept the 'ohana intact.

This pragmatism helped Luján accommodate the rigid schedules of the plantations. The sugar plantations worked from six in the morning to two thirty in the afternoon because of the hot weather. By now, Samuel Ho'olohekamohoali'i had moved from being the sugar sampler into becoming the plantation *kikola* (timekeeper). This was a plum job for a kanaka. But it was demanding, and it allowed no mistakes. To get this job, you had to be up at four in the morning, be in the fields at 5:00 a.m., get full work teams for the *luna* ("overseer"), handle the time cards, and deal with having teams large enough to work the fields set for that day. The plantation was large, and Samuel Ho'olohekamohoali'i had to get to every field on horseback. He got his work done and was usually home at two thirty in the afternoon.

Childhood photo taken in the corn fields on the Lujan farm and ranch. From left to right: Herman, Kenneth and Leilani.

Samuel Ho'olohekamohoali'i had four children. The first was stillborn. Then came Kaleoaloha (Kenneth), Leilehua (Herman), and Leilani (Alice). I was the middle child. Kaleo was seven years older, and Leilani was thirteen months younger. Our full names were Kenneth Dennis Kaleoaloha Lujan, Herman Damien Leilehua Lujan, and Alice Maris Leilani Lujan. I was named after Father Damien the Leper Priest and St. Herman Joseph on whose Catholic saint's day I was born, April 7, 1936.

As I grew up, I used to wait for my father when he rode home from work. I would wait for him at the head of the driveway to the family house. Samuel Ho'olohekamohoali'i usually stopped at the Honohina Store to get a treat for his waiting son. I could hear the horse from almost a mile away. Only today, the sound of the hooves was different as Samuel Ho'olohekamohoali'i had a different horse at full trot on the paved Old Government Road.

Samuel Ho'olohekamohoali'i came over the rise in the road, and I could not stop myself. I ran to meet my dad and the different horse. I got to see the horse as my dad dismounted. Eating my treat, I gave the horse the once-over and realized that this was a new horse! It was a pure white horse, and it stood fifteen hands. So I hugged my dad and thanked him for the usual dried mango treat and began to praise him for getting a new horse. My dad calmed me down and beckoned to me to come to the head of the driveway and to wait a moment. I was puzzled, but I did as I was asked. Then up the rise, there appeared not a horse—as I had expected the old horse would be kept—but a car, a white pickup. The driver was the plantation manager, Mr. John M. Ross. Mr. Ross had a brand new car! We chatted briefly about the car, and Mr. Ross gave me my usual candy treat. I thanked him and as the manager pulled away, it dawned on me. Mr. Ross had gotten a new pickup. He gave his white horse to Samuel Ho'olohekamohoali'i. It was a new car for an old horse! Just then, there was a horn toot. It was head overseer Henry Weber. He was driving Ross's old pickup. Weber, the German, got the used pickup, and the kanaka Samuel *Ho'olohekamohoali'i* got the used horse. It was the horse trade of all time!

The 'ohana grew as Alice bore her four children. The first was stillborn. And in 1929, she gave birth to Kenneth Dennis Kaleoaloha Lujan. He was a handsome child, and he grew in good looks as his book of time grew in years. His inoa was apt. It translated as "the voice of love." By now, Alice was a teacher working for her father at O'okala School; she was living with Lucas Lujan, Sammy and baby Kaleo, and all the other members of the extended 'ohana still at home.

While Alice was having her children, Hawai'i was suffering severely from the epidemics that swept the 'aina. When Alice lost baby Lujan in 1926, six Lujans died in or before their teens. Most died from tuberculosis or related illnesses and two from leprosy. Lacking immunity, the illnesses introduced by the European and American immigrants were lethal. Many were sailors who were world travelers. Others were the paniolo and the imported plantation workers. The early plantation workers brought their families, as Ignacio had. But the Japanese, Chinese, and Filipino workers came as bachelors. And they found gratification among the women of paradise, leaving a wake of wretched pandemic illnesses behind. Kaililau herself would succumb to complications from tuberculosis and heart disease in 1914. Lujan was seventy and decimated by his loss.

The period from 1848 (Mahele) to annexation (*ho'oku'i*) in 1898 was not only a time of political and socioeconomic change but also a time of profound cultural change. The Christianization of the people made morality a driving force in civilizing the kanaka. To Christianize was to civilize. To civilize was to industrialize. And in the American version, to industrialize was the moral imperative. It was known as the Doctrine of Manifest Destiny. The doctrine said that it was a moral obligation to Christianize non-Christians and that the Christians should use wealth as a tool. This ethic brought the Industrial Revolution from America to Hawai'i. Annexation was the sign of its success. Here, as elsewhere, sitting governments were moved out of the way; and in the name of democracy, political and social systems were built to replace them. Baptize and build became the rallying cry of the moguls of the nineteenth century.

Chapter Six

Shaping Change

Ke Kalai

The blight was devastating to kanaka religion, language, land, wealth, and political power. Cultures facing such profound pruning of the society in such a short time did not usually survive. Lujan had the foresight to send the family to school to educate them for dealing with the next wave of change after annexation. Kaililau saved and even expanded the ʻaina, all while others lost their lands. The Ignacios had the artful skill and perception to be the educators for change. Alice pursued a teaching degree from normal school while Samuel Hoʻolohekamohoaliʻi waited for the empty saddle to begin his education. These choices showed a capacity to sculpt change by using education to gain the skills to overcome the blight and by "Hawaiianizing" the evolving culture with an under layer of Hawaiian values and beliefs. The by word was *i mua*—forward!

You could see it in the reintroduction of the *hula* by King David Kalakaua. It was there in the music of the era. You heard it in the music composed by the last of the monarchs, King David Kalakaua and Queen Liliuokalani. Both were prodigious composers. The church choirs and services were keeping the *himeni* alive. Students were going from school to their music lessons. Others were heading to practice at the *hula halau* with the *kumu hula* (hula teacher). Boys were taking hula since the hula was not meant for women only.

Chant (*oli*) was the ladder of history for a people rich in oral traditions but with no writing tools to record the kanaka culture and history. The emergence of chant signaled the rebirth of kanaka traditions and ways of living. These cultural practices marked the rebirth of tradition. When taken together, all signaled the revitalizing and infusion of the spiritual and other values of *Ka Po'e Kahiko*, the people of times past, into the collision of ongoing cultural change. Both personal and individual spiritual values on the one hand and group and social subcultures on the other were interlayered, sculpting the emerging Hawai'i at *ho'okui*, annexation. While business leadership, social leadership, and workers in the mills and ranches of Hawai'i were all being pushed into the twentieth century, the tie to the past was also growing.

Exemplary of this were the stories told by the elders. One of these I remember involves Pele, the goddess of fire. Pele was supposed to have come upon a lover, a fellow named Kamapua'a, a red pig demigod. They fell in love, and Pele was elated. But Kamapua'a betrayed her, and she went into a rage. She took Kamapua'a to the river at Waianuenue on the north edge of Hilo and chased him across the river to Pu'ueo on the other side of the river. She then struck a bargain with him. She would keep him safe from lava (she being the demigoddess of fire) so long as he never crossed the river. To this day, those who remember the tales of old have accepted the idea that the land north of Waianuenue would be free from lava flows. To this date, that has been the case.

There are also tales of Pele in the villages around Waianuenue. In addition to Pu'ueo Village, there are Ha'aheo, Wainaku, Honoli'i, and Papaikou. There are also varying tales about this, but the common view is that there was an old lady, a *luahine*. She wandered aimlessly looking for Kamapua'a. At night, she prowled the roads. There were two main roads in this area—the Old Government Road where Wainaku was and the Mamalahoa Highway, which was Hawai'i's main road. All the other places named were on Mamalahoa Highway. A plantation worker named Sunichi "Wimpy" Sugino swore that while driving north toward Papaikou one evening at around ten o'clock, he was stopped by a *luahine* wandering down the highway, crossing in and out of the road. Her shadow was fetching, so he stopped. When he rolled the window down, the lady's face aged into ugliness on the spot. She reached into the car to touch him. Frightened out of his wits, he hit the gas and sped away. To his passing, Sugino swore by his story.

Another layer of new over old is in the customs surrounding the volcanoes. The Big Island is dominated geologically and socially by the Kilauea *lua,* Kilauea crater. Halemaumau is the largest and most accessible of the Kilauea calderas. People are attracted by the eruptions. But local custom calls for particular ways to approach Pele. The tradition is to bring her food of some sort as a gift. In the Lujan 'ohana, the custom was to drive to the overlook at Halemaumau Crater. We would gather berries, except for the 'ohelo kau la'au berry, and we cast them in to Pele. This would protect us from her wrath.

Because of epidemics and the lack of immunity among kanakas, most kanaka families had a concern for health. Many of these families saw both a western family physician (*kauka*) and a naturopathic physician (*kahuna lapa'au*). Among the better known of the *kahuna lapa'au* were the Kaonohe brothers. They were based in Honolulu, but they came to Kona once a month to treat their patients on the Big Island. The Lujan 'ohana would drive to Kona from Peleau to see Dr. Alexander Kaonohe. Samuel Ho'olohekamohoali'i would be treated for diabetes with herbs. I was the asthmatic in the family. I got cactus leaf boiled and mashed like poi. It was the "asthma cocktail." It was awful. But when taken, mucus began to be expelled and wheezing stopped. The diabetes which plagued Samuel Ho'olohekamohoali'i was countered by a kauka, a regular doctor (actually, he was the plantation doctor), Dr Bill Bergin. Sam's diabetes was also being treated by the 'ohelo kau la'au tea prescribed by the *kahuna lapa'au*. The shrub is of the cranberry family, and it grows in the volcano ash. The 'ohana made regular trips to the volcano to collect the 'ohelo kau la'au shrub whose leaves and stalks were then boiled into a strong tea. So a kahuna and a kauka provided double coverage when folks were ill. It was a way of coping with change.

Kanakas have a long standing tradition about spirits. Each 'ohana has a spirit that guides it, much like the totems of Alaska natives. Kanaka fate is tied to the sea. We were a seafaring people. We discovered Hawai'i in our sailings, probably on a discovery expedition. These islands were larger than the Marquesas, our original home islands in Polynesia. The food to survive and the wood to repair their canoes were there. We rebuilt the canoes and returned to our homeland in the South Pacific regaling the adventure and the discovery of the place named Hawai'i. We digress here to make the point that seafaring, fishing, and focusing on the ocean were habits of culture for the Lujan 'ohana. And for the 'ohana, the spirit world gave meaning to the values and experiences of the sea.

The Lujan ʻaumakua was the shark (*mano*). Lujan tutored young Samuel Hoʻolohekamohoaliʻi about the things of the sea. For example, when throwing net or pole fishing, always face the sea. Count the waves, paying attention to waves five through seven. They are the strongest waves and will hurt or kill if ignored. When fishing, especially when throwing net, always pick the smallest fish and throw them back into the sea; symbolically, it is as food for the ʻaumakua, but practically, it is to not deplete the stock of fish by consuming its young. Catch fish without hurting the fish.

In the ʻAuwapuhi Stream, catfish were not to be fished by pole or by regular net. Instead, we were to creep slowly up stream, so the fish could not easily slip away with the current. We were to find a natural pool area in the stream and block it off with stones. The sap of the hau tree is intoxicating to smaller fish. So we lanced the hau bark and drained the white milky sap, muddling it into a paste. The fish would ingest the muddled hau sap. We put it in the water to make the fish lose their balance. Once they were out of balance, the fish were plucked by hand, leaving the young to swim for another day.

Practices that relate to the sea also relate to forests. It is widely known that the oʻo bird was prized for the single yellow feather under each wing. Too many birds would have to die to make a lei or other ornament involving feathers. So the kanaka devised a scheme to get around that. The milk of the *ulu* (breadfruit) is very sticky. A paste of it was smeared on tree branches where the oʻo landed to feed. The birds would get stuck on the branch. The bird was then caught by hand, and its two feathers were plucked. The bird was then cleaned and released.

In addition to rules about the land and how to live on it in harmony, there were also rules that applied to kanaka and their social harmony. The use of language as a tool for social harmony is especially important in the naming, inoa, of a person. As Alice bore children, inoa became important. Foremost among the rules was the expectation that names of others should not be borrowed without permission. Names should not be used because they sounded nice or were frivolous. Kenneth Dennis Kaleoaloha was born in 1929. Samuel Ho'olohekamohoali'i and Alice then had Herman Damien Leilehua in 1936 and Alice Maris Leilani Lujan in 1937. Kenneth sired one daughter, Kuulei, who was raised by a stepfather. She had a child. I had three children. I adopted the two children of my wife, Carla Wayne Williams—Laura Gwendolyn and Mark Duane. Carla and I had a son named Timothy Samuel Lujan, named after my father.

Timothy Samuel sired two boys: Timothy S. Lehua "TJ" Lujan and Cody Kahikolu Lujan. Among these names, the *lehua* name is prominent. I was named Herman Damien Leilehua and was born on the day of celebration for the Roman Catholic saint Herman Joseph. *Damien* refers to the leper priest of Kalaupapa. *Leilehua* is my inoa. *Lehua* is the flower of the ohia tree. A lei of the lehua celebrates a beloved sibling of the 'ohana. Timothy Samuel Lehua "TJ" Lujan also refers to the ohia tree and flower that stretches west from Lehua Island near Ni'ihau to the sunsets of the eastern Hawai'i skies. Together these images imply someone who brings inclusiveness to the 'ohana. *Kahikolu* is the kanaka name of Cody Lujan. *Kahikolu* refers to the Trinity of the Christian religion. *Kahikolu* in this case is the bringing together of his father, mother Dana Dixon, and stepbrother Timothy Lehua (TJ) into a new family. This translates into "the one who ties everyone together".

Alice Maris Leilani Lujan is a unique name. *Maris* is the Latin root word for the sea, and *Leilani* is the heavenly flower. In her case, the name implies great beauty stretching across the seas. She had four sons: Kevin, Kenneth, Keithan, and Kristian.

As the family grew, Samuel Ho'olohekamohoali'i managed to find time for himself. He was a great athlete. In high school he was named All-Star Left Tackle for the Territory of Hawaii's all-star football team. But he also loved baseball. He was the star of the Hakalau Plantation All Stars. He played second base and pitched. He was ambidextrous. He pitched with the same arm as the opposing hitter used. So he pitched with his right hand to right-handed batters and his left hand to left-handed batters. Opponents were always aggravated by the switch pitcher from Hakalau. He also was a switch hitter at the plate and swung a good bat, winning games for Hakalau on the mound, at the plate, and on the base.

While the 'ohana grew, and the times changed, there were groups and organizations actively keeping traditions alive, especially as the generations changed and the number of blood kanakas diminished to a few thousand. Most notable among these for the Lujan 'ohana was the Sons of Kamehameha. It was a brotherhood of blood kanakas who kept the culture alive. Samuel Ho'olohekamohoali'i was active in it until his passing. When he did pass in 1969, only four Sons of Kamehameha were active in the order! As they chanted their prayer at his funeral, it was a dirge of desperation and the silence of hope fading away.

Chapter Seven

The State

Ka Moku'aina

The decades from 1898, *ho'o hui 'aina* (annexation) to 1958, *ka moku'aina* (statehood), marked an era of great immigration and profound economic and cultural change for the children of the kanaka of the twentieth century. There were two sources of the new *haole* (foreigner). The first was the fundamental shift in the economy through tourism; the other was the number of soldiers who passed through Hawai'i during the *kekauahonua*, the Second World War, and were taken by *kanaka* culture. They were called *haole*, a term that meant more than foreigner. As Kupuna Abraham Pi'ianai'a observed, *ha* meant with breath, and *'ole* meant without it. *Kupuna* (elder) would convey and pass on the care of the 'ohana to a member selected by the kupuna by breathing upon the fontanel of the chosen one. Those who were not given breath were called *haole* or "without the breath of the 'ohana."

The Lujan 'ohana grew after the wedding of Sam and Alice, as locals called them. But that growth brought cultural difference to the surface with all of its conflicts and contradictions. Augusta Cambra, the Portuguese, and Lucas Lujan, the Spanish, were cordial with each other but nothing more. Samuel Ho'olohekamohoali'i was not the choice Augusta would have made for Alice. When Alice eloped, the wrath of Augusta cast a pall over the 'ohana. Augusta would not speak to Alice for seven years. And then one Saturday at confession the catholic priest, Father Gabrial Feron, refused her absolution unless she broke the silence and spoke to her daughter. Augusta did, and through life, Alice had a cool but respectful relationship with her mother. It warmed up after Samuel Ho'olohekamohoali'i gave Amos Joaquin and Augusta Cambra Ignacio a one acre house lot for $1 on which they built their dream house. Nevertheless, Amos Joaquin and Samuel Ho'olohekamohoali'i were always healing conflicts beneath the surface. You would think that Augusta had learned something from the conflict. But as Lucas Lujan would grouse, the Spanish have a saying for it. Augusta Cambra Ignacio was a *duena de la casa*, the ruler of the household. She often did what she wished when she wished.

This willfulness to have her way surfaced when her son Clarence decided to marry. Clarence had joined the navy, and while on shore, he met Mabel Serile, a beautiful Filipina teenager. When Mabel was seventeen, Clarence, in his twenties, proposed. When Clarence brought her to meet the family, Augusta would not speak or be cordial to young Mabel. Augusta Cambra wanted her out of the house. However, the romance had its own tempo which did not include a veto by Augusta Cambra.

The wedding was taking place anyway. It was planned that when the wedding day came, Augusta Cambra would ride with Alice,

Sammy, and their children to attend. They were to leave at 1:00 p.m. Well, one o'clock came and went as did each minute beyond. Finally at 1:15 p.m., having called across the yard to Augusta's house, Sammy drove from his house to her driveway; he parked the car there, left the engine running, walked up to her door, and called for her to come. She refused, he asked again, and she still refused. Then Sammy let loose his booming timekeeper voice, "Mama, if you don't come out, I am coming in to pick you up and carry you to the car. It is Clarence's wedding, and you are his mother. So I am coming in now."

Well, folks did not talk to her like that, especially a son-in-law. But she knew he meant what he said. So she pouted her way to the car. At the reception, she refused to get out of the car again. Sammy looked at her, "Mama, not again," he said quietly and directly. He took her by the arm and marched her to the party.

By now, Alice was teaching at O'okala School, where Amos Joaquin was principal. Kaleoaloha was one year old. Back in the classroom, she felt she needed more information and skills to teach classes that were increasing in size and more culturally diverse. Culturally mixed classes meant linguistically mixed students and a growing number of students without English as their first language. English was being displaced by *Pinoi* (Filipinos) with three dialects—Ilocano, Visayan, and Tagalog. In addition, there were Japanese, Okinawan, Portuguese, and Puerto Rican all in the same class. She talked with Sammy about her frustration and broached the idea of going to college in Honolulu at the University of Hawai'i. In the summer of 1930, Alice set off for Honolulu and the university to get a degree in education. For seventeen years, she left the three children with Sammy every summer and went to Honolulu. Even during World War II, she went to get that degree. In 1947, she graduated from the University of Hawai'i.

To celebrate in the kanaka way, Samuel Ho'olohekamohoali'i threw a big *luau* (feast). Relatives and friends from everywhere came, nearly a hundred in number. It was so large that the family had to rent the Hakalau School Gymnasium. As was the custom, Samuel Ho'olohekamohoali'i rose to toast Alice and her degree. He did not drink, but on this occasion, he poured a shot glass of pure Four Roses whiskey and toasted his beloved. With all glasses dry, he asked Alice what she wanted to do next. She had not talked much with Sammy about it, but she said she had a new goal. She wanted to leave Peleau Village for two years and go to New York City to get a master's degree at Columbia University, Barnard College of Education, to specialize in teaching speech and reading. Asked when by Sammy, she answered, "This year."

And so it was that the man who dreamed of chemistry and college would instead support his wife when she would get into a Douglass DC-4 aircraft and fly to New York on a four prop plane, flying for around twenty hours. Meanwhile he raised the children while she completed her graduated studies with a master's degree in education from Barnard College. He then hocked the family lands and bought a new 1948 Packard as her gift and flew from Hilo to Honolulu to Detroit to pick up the Packard. He then drove to pick her up in New York, and they spent the summer visiting forty of the forty-eight states!

Photo of Alice and Samuel Lujan take with family car.

In California, they were on a special mission. Samuel Ho'olohekamohoali'i had a younger brother, Lucas P. Lujan, who left home for California some thirty years before; Sam wanted to find him to reconnect with the 'ohana. Lucas had not been in touch, and it bothered Samuel Ho'olohekamohoali'i. Samuel Ho'olohekamohoali'i had one lead after calling relatives and checking California phone books. It was that Lucas P. was an auto mechanic in the Bay Area. So Samuel Ho'olohekamohoali'i decided he and Alice would drive from dealer to dealer until they found Lucas P.

They started near their motel in Berkeley. A car dealer was a few blocks away. Samuel Ho'olohekamohoali'i parked his car and went to the service department inquiring if anyone knew a mechanic named Lucas P. Lujan. The manager said no, but he said there was a Sam Lujan working there as a mechanic. The manager pointed to a car with a mechanic lying underneath it.

Samuel Hoʻolohekamohoaliʻi walked over to the car and said, "I am looking for a Sam Lujan. Are you Sam Lujan?"

Lucas P. said, "Yes."

"I am Sam. You are Lucas," Sam replied. "Who gave you permission to use my name, anyway?" Samuel Hoʻolohekamohoaliʻi was steaming. But Alice entered the service area and cooled Samuel Hoʻolohekamohoaliʻi down. They visited with Lucas for a day or so and headed home to Peleau.

And what happened to Alice? She went back into the classroom for a while and then became the specialist on reading and speech for the whole island of Hawaiʻi!

And what about Samuel Hoʻolohekamohoaliʻi? Well, he quit the plantation in 1948 and devoted himself to sugarcane planting and cattle ranching on the Lujan ʻaina. His new career as an independent cane planter and rancher gave him time to drive Alice to the outlying schools where they would stay in the teacher's cottage. While she taught, he would fish for dinner, visit friends, and read. Or he would walk the lands of his ancestors and be free to be himself.

In the midst of all these changes, the Second World War exploded over Pearl Harbor in Honolulu, blasting molten steel, mangling sinking ships, spraying burning oil across the adjacent land, and giving a new definition to a six-alarm fire.

It was otherwise a typical Sunday morning for the Lujan ʻohana. Sam and Alice were readying themselves for 7:30 mass at Ninole Catholic Church. Kaleo and Leilani were also suiting up for mass. But I was not getting dressed. I spent the night gasping with asthma and was whipped by this first asthma attack in my life. I turned on the radio to listen to *Hawaiʻi Calls*, a radio show with Webley Edwards. The show was broadcast from the Ala Moana Hotel, one of the hotels in Waikiki; it involved news, commentary, and music.

At right around 7:00 a.m., Edwards broke into the song being broadcast. His voice booming across the airwaves, he cried out, "The planes you see are not on maneuvers. This is real! This is war! The Japanese are bombing Honolulu at Pearl Harbor! Take cover and remain tuned!" He then proceeded to give blow-by-blow accounts of the bombing and strafing of Barbers Point and Hickam Field. And the war was directly striking the 'ohana. Uncle Albert Ignacio was a pipefitter at Pearl Harbor. He was ordered in and went speeding from his home on Beretania Street through Honolulu's surface streets to Pearl Harbor. He was trying to beat the bombing and find an open gate at the base. He made it and was immediately sent to repair the salvageable ships, some still on crackling fire. The firefighters needed water, and the plumbers were there to get it. The heat was hellacious. The task was daunting. And there would be more ships sinking than floating in the harbor. Albert would be lucky to come out alive, and he was.

Directly across Pearl Harbor naval base was *Makuahine* (Aunty) Rose Farm's home. It was right on the water. They had a pier. And every Sunday morning, *kaukini* (cousin) Jimmy Farm was out on the pier crabbing for Sunday brunch. And so he was on this Sunday. Thirteen-year-old Jimmy sat on the pier watching the actual battle. Around 7:15 or so, he heard an engine sputtering and a plane trailing flame as it descended toward the family barn. He turned to run home past the barn and saw the plane heading straight for it. As he reached the barn, he watched the plane crash. He ran toward the plane and could see the pilot trying to get out. But the pilot could not open the cockpit. Jimmy could not help him, and he stoically watched him burn to death. As the pilot stopped screaming, and his body began to turn into jelly, Jimmy was traumatized by the experience. In a week or so, he began to lose his hair. He remained bald for the rest of his life. In addition, kaukini Jimmy stopped speaking generally and spoke only to Samuel Ho'olohekamohoali'i.

It happened that Samuel Ho'olohekamohoali'i needed help on the farm and ranch. So he talked with kaukini Jimmy and Makuakine Rose Farm about having kaukini Jimmy come to Peleau and work on the farm and ranch. Samuel Ho'oholekamohoali'i needed assistance in fencing the cattle paddocks as he was starting his new ranching endeavor upon his retirement from the plantation. After some thinking, kaukini Jimmy agreed. Within a few weeks, he arrived at Peleau. He slowly began to overcome his speaking impediment and grew comfortable living with the 'ohana. He was a hard worker, and he regained his self-respect. However, his selective speechlessness was never understood.

While Albert was fighting fires, and Jimmy was watching the pains of war unfold, a car pulled into the Lujan driveway at Peleau. Samuel Ho'olohekamohoali'i and Alice and Kaleo and Leilani were just home from church and were getting out of the Lujan car. Two Shinto (Japanese priests) approached, and Samuel Ho'olohekamohoali'i recognized them as they were plantation workers. He greeted them coolly for they were robed in their priestly attire that was very colorful but a bit off-putting. They greeted Samuel Ho'olohekamohoali'i politely. Samuel Ho'olohekamohoali'i returned the good morning. They were reassuring him that the Lujan 'ohana should not be afraid. When the Japanese soldiers arrived, the Japanese were going to treat people with respect, especially Sam-san, as Samuel Ho'olohekamohoali'i was known among the Japanese plantation workers. Sam-san thanked them for their concern. He indicated that there would be no occupation of Hawai'i Island to his knowledge and urged them to go home and remain there for their own safety, as animosity regarding the Japanese was already present in the plantation camps.

By noon, the government was being organized. Not having the status of a state, Lieutenant General Richardson—head of the army in Hawai'i—was taking command, and martial law was declared. Basically, the sitting governor—an appointee of the president—was under the authority of the general. With the war taking place in Hawai'i, defense of the islands was the focus of this new wartime junta. Some Japanese who were community leaders were taken in for interviews, and some were sent to concentration camps. There were no camps on the island of Hawai'i. The Big Island had the largest Japanese settlements due to the plantations and their roles in the war. Besides, these Japanese were largely apolitical, especially those who were not citizens. They proved, however, to be very loyal as the war unfolded.

Community leaders were contacted and brought in for setting up the defense of the island. The worry was over submarines as one-person subs had been built and tested and were deployed by the Japanese. One was even believed to have been captured.

The line of defense would begin along the shores of the windward side of the Big Island. Hawai'i had many gulches, valleys, and beaches. This was ideal for submarine landings. The Hilo Consolidated Railroad went from Hilo to Honoka'a with bridges all along the way. It would be the backbone of defense for the Big Island. Two soldiers with appropriate arms would patrol the railroad trestles, one pair per gulch. Civilian leaders would provide support, especially those who knew the plantation road grids. The island was carved into sections that were called blocks. Each block had a block warden who would coordinate their activity. The wardens were to do nightly checks.

Wardens would also bring food for the troops to be distributed during the block warden stops.

Samuel Ho'olohekamohoali'i was an obvious choice for block warden. As *kikola* (plantation timekeeper), he knew the roads everywhere and was also highly respected by the locals including the Japanese. In addition to being the *kikola* and working from four in the morning to two o'clock in the afternoon, he would do the farm chores. The 'ohana had several hundred chickens and about a hundred pigs. They were a challenge.

So were his new night duties. As the sun began to set, Samuel Ho'olohekamohoali'i would fill his 1937 Dodge station wagon with gasoline and head for the cane fields. At nights, he looked for signal lights from the shore or ships and relayed the information to the soldiers on patrol.

Because he was block warden, Samuel Ho'olohekamohoali'i received an A ration allocation for gasoline, the largest allotment available to a civilian. He also had to paint and shield his headlights. So he attached a visor to the top half of the light and painted the light red. That had the light pointing to the road for near visibility. He also had to carry a gas mask, a helmet, and a rifle. He carried his personal twelve-gauge shotgun.

Everyone was issued a gas mask. Each Friday, while at school, everyone had to don their mask for a drill and walk through the library or gym where gas had been deployed. When anyone heard an airplane and was outdoors, that person had to drop to the ground and lie flat. There was a 4:00 p.m. curfew for those in their teens and under. Others had a firm curfew at 7:00 p.m. People like block wardens had no curfew. Bus schedules had to be changed. Students still managed to bring humor into this. The gas masks were used as bases when they played baseball!

As block warden, Samuel Ho'olohekamohoali'i saw how grave things could become. News of air raids in Europe only fanned the flames of worry. So he decided that we would build a bomb shelter near the house. It was about twelve by fifteen and over six feet deep, so all could stand in it. Gas masks, food, and health emergency needs such as bandages were stocked. With power to the shelter, the radio was available for the news.

Living in a time of war is more than frightening. It places a shadow over everything. From sunrise to sunset, time is structured, and you live with it. You get used to the sense of being watched. The alternative is less desirable. For the Japanese at the plantation camps, there was the added pall of suspicion. Were they "Japanese," as we historically called them here in Hawai'i, or were they "Japs," part of the language of new patriotism, spawning words and vocabulary to deliver the new content of war and treason? The Japanese suffered from the latter. They were sped into concentration camps. Some were sent to camps in California. By contrast, while all the cleansing of Japanese was being carried out, Germans were never even shadowed. Henry Weber, the local plantation overseer of German descent was ipso facto okay and free from this animosity. Territory of Hawai'i senator Tommy Sakakihara, who was Japanese, was not. He was in custody while being interrogated.

It is worth noting here that the Germans were prominent in trading goods and dry goods and haberdashery businesses in Hawai'i. On an island where everything comes from far away, the purveyors of basic goods thrived. You see these judgmental differences, and you learn quickly in war to be sparing in speech, to be careful with written words, and to see no one as a friend to trust until they earn it. This was neatly captured in the presumed aphorism, plastered on US savings bonds, "Loose lips sink ships!"

The Lujan 'ohana was very active in the war at home. Samuel Ho'olohekamohoali'i was the busy block warden. He used to take one child on patrol from time to time. These were exciting rides at night, weaving through the cane fields and feeding the troops at the trestles and gulches. As timekeeper for the plantation, he knew the roads so well from riding them every day that he often drove with his lights out. Leilani and I loved the spookiness of it all. It was our ride with the ghosts—the *'aumakua*!

Alice was leading the Future Farmers of America (FFA) and the 4-H clubs at Ninole School. These had youth programs in agriculture and citizenship as part of the community level war effort.

John Kaukokalani Purdy, widower of Sussanah Lujan, was the most prominent of all the locals. The US Marines were looking for a headquarters site. He built a large home in the heart of Waimea and was one of the senior paniolos at the Parker Ranch. The 1st and 2nd Marine Corps Divisions were stationing themselves for encampment in the Waimea and Pohakuloa areas near the slopes of Mauna Kea. John's personal home was quite ample. John had horses and was the lead horse tender for Parker Ranch. So he built a tack house behind the big house for the saddles and other riding equipment he used such as shoes and tacks for shoeing. He thought he would live there as the marines started their horse trading with him over the sequestering. The discussions did not last long.

John got his price; now a widower, he was satisfied with the tack house since he spent most of his spare time there working the *'awe'awe* (horse saddle tree and ties). He loved to sit there after dinner, sipping from his shot glass of bourbon and "talking story" about whatever topic came to mind or teaching the young ones by answering their curiosity through weaving tales, both true and apocryphal. In either case, he embellished his tales to keep the story talking alive in their dreams and their reminiscences of the tales he told.

There was a ringer, however, in the arrangement. Sussana had died and left him a stepchild. She was Susie Purdy. She was in her early teens. All John needed was a pubescent early teenager unsupervised all day with her stepfather out on the range and miles from home. Add to this menu of issues two whole marine divisions of single men, and no one needs the painted picture of what would come next. John also felt out of saddle on raising a teenager. Put it all together, and it spelled Alice and Sam in that order. So Alice and Sam came to the rescue! They drove to Waimea with an empty backseat in Sam's 1937 Dodge station wagon and returned with it full of Susie, her clothes, and her cosmetics. It was the cosmetics that would keep Alice and Sam worried.

The marines, however, tended to get their girl. If we could keep the girl from the boys by taking her away from the boys, the boys would likely find a way to get their girl by other means. Susie was fifty miles from any marines. But the marines had jeeps and trucks and the road around the island, the Old Government Road. It went right by the front door of the 'ohana home. And the marines had a practice of stopping at local residences to fill their water cans. Well, you can guess. Within a few weeks, there was a line of water cans from the spigot to the road. Susie's marines had found their girl. For much of the war, that would continue until the local boys decided they needed to fix that.

The many convoys from Hilo to Waimea stopped regularly at Peleau to refill water containers and snack on the many fruits in the 'ohana home's yard. Several of these Marines became friends, and they spent their days off at the house. They were fed a good and traditional kanaka barbecue cooked on keawe wood (a desert tree) and quantities of beer. Brian Judge of Georgia and Frank Tirico from New Jersey were the regulars, and they brought buddies with them. Their connection with the 'ohana was such that when Sam and Alice took their tour of forty of the forty-eight states on the US mainland, they visited and were hosted by the marines they had befriended.

Food rationing was a constant condition of war. So was losing marines the 'ohana had come to know. Upon returning from Tarawa, Guadalcanal, and Saipan, about twenty marines the 'ohana came to know were killed. It was tough for Sam and Alice's children. This was further traumatizing when members of the 442nd Army Division began to come home maimed and battered. Many of the young soldiers had Alice as their teacher. The soldiers would always check in with her when on furlough. It was all heartbreaking for Alice.

The war brought profound changes to Hawaii's people. The population grew as war created jobs, especially in Honolulu. Labor began to organize, first with the longshoremen and then with the plantation workers. The issue hit the 'ohana. Amos Andrew Ignacio, Alice's eldest brother, was the leader needed in the territory legislature to lift wages from about fifty cents per hour to $1.25 an hour. He was among the negotiators in the bargaining, and he became widely known in the International Longshore and Warehousemen's Union, the ILWU.

Harry Bridges from California was the union leader and was one of the most successful spokespersons for the ILWU. He was also accused of being a communist. He had friends in the Communist Party who were supporters of the ILWU, and this complicated the struggle for unionization and later for statehood in Hawai'i. The five largest plantations known as the "Big Five" used injunctions versus strikes and pushed the communist label to undermine the union movement. Amos Andrew was soon to be in the midst of it as he had just been elected to the House of Representative of the Territory of Hawai'i. He was the first union leader so elected. He was a successful organizer and one the Big Five plantations had come to respect. He left the legislature after several sessions to become the manager, *wiliko*, of Honoka'a Sugar Mill.

Chapter Eight

From Sickle to Blade

Mai Pahikeke'e I Palaulau

The war years brought with them production techniques pushed by the government's demand for speed in the war supply chain. The resulting American production methods revolutionized manufacturing. Mass production hit the labor market like a ton of bricks and mortar. The progress of the war led industry to move from human to technological methods of growth. In the field, it boiled down to moving from the plantation worker and the hand-wielded sickle to the tractor with the automatic cutting blade. Mules and flumes were moved out, and trucks pulling single or double trailers replaced them. The revolution was quick and deep. Within months, camps were emptied, workers were laid off, and plantations were merging. Most mills went dead and were bought up by sugar producers elsewhere in the world. The field hands were paid a severance fee, and the plantation offered them newly built homes they could buy from the plantation at modest prices. One of the first was built in Pepe'ekeo for the workers of the C. Brewer Company of San Francisco.

Samuel Ho'olohekamohoali'i could see the change affecting most of the top management jobs, including the *kikolo*. Most of the overseers would be let go and one of the mills would likely service all the mills from Pepe'ekeo. The technology was more mobile than the people; that, combined with the lack of education beyond middle and high school, made the locals a liability. The irony was evident to everyone. Just as labor organized to get living wages in Hawai'i, the industry put its money on mechanization and automation. Even Amos Andrew faced that buzz saw and viewed it as a way out, taking the job as *wiliko* (manager) at the Honoka'a Mill.

So in 1948, after more than twenty-five years at the plantation, Samuel Ho'olohekamohoali'i left the Hakalau Plantation Company for ranching and independent cane planting. As you might guess, he helped those he could who shared his years at the Honohina Sugar Company (bought by the Hakalau Sugar Company). He hired several who worked under him—Mr. and Mrs. Tsuja, Mrs. Isa, and Mrs. Oba, all from Okinawa, and a Filipino named Ramon Saucedo. These helped him with the cane crops as they knew the business backward and forward. He also hired kaukini Jimmy Farm to help him with the cattle. Samuel Ho'olohekamohoali'i also had a hundred rabbits, two hundred Leghorn chickens, fifty Duroc Jersey and Yorkshire pigs, plus two hundred acres with several hundred head of cattle, mostly Polled Herefords. He stocked some of his cattle from the Parker Ranch through John Purdy. It was hard work, but it was his to work, so Samuel Ho'olohekamohoali'i moved with speed and good joy into his second career.

He was new to ranching, so he got help from the University of Hawai'i agriculture extension specialists. The issue for Samuel

Ho'olohekamohoali'i was efficiency. If machines and technology could eliminate his traditional experience and job, then new ways could be found to help him in his second career. Using the chemistry he learned as the plantation chemist, he ran soil samples, tracked water flow, analyzed soil content and erosion, and experimented with high nutrition grasses. Cattle breeds were researched to find the breed that fared best in the hot and humid conditions of Peleau. The results were compellingly instructive. The soil was acidic, and it needed lime to stabilize itself. Water was ample, but the terrain was eroding as water moved quickly with no cane stumps in the way to slow the flow of water. Diversion ditches could be dug to slow the flow of the water and make it feed the soil as it meandered along the streams and gulches to the sea.

The best fit breed was the Polled Hereford, the breed he had. This breed had large stomachs and could hold a lot of feed. In Peleau, the rain was full and frequent, so the cattle were consuming as much water as nutrient. And they were roaming large paddocks and eating the tastiest grass, leaving weeds and bare spots in their wake. The resolution? Cut the land into five-acre paddocks. Fence them and make the cattle eat the grass down evenly before they moved on. By creating paddocks in five-acre parcels, he could rotate the herd through and return them to the original paddock with the grass ready for grazing again.

Photo of Samuel Lujan at the Lujan farm and ranch
taken with the cattle he talked to every day.

The last item was the grass itself. The grass varied widely in nutrients. So the agriculture specialists looked the world over for climates like Peleau and then studied grass characteristics. They discovered a grass that fit the bill in Africa. It was called Pangola, and it provided ample nutrition in spite of the rains of Peleau. The grass was known for its long runners that helped the grass recover from intensive grazing.

If you think that Samuel Ho'olohekamohoali'i was going to stop there, well, he was not. His pigs were also a concern. He had popular breeds, but he had no food plan to improve growth naturally. After tests with local sources for fruits, vegetables, and grasses, Samuel Ho'olohekamohoali'i came up with a new approach. He bought a used five-hundred-gallon steel container from the plantation (they were dismantling the mills) to cook fresh slop every day. The slop had a base of fruits and vegetables. There were usually breadfruit, mango, guava, and bananas, all available for this *kuleana* (property) stew.

The unused remains of slaughtered cattle were added, and the resulting stew was topped with molasses for sugar and flavor. He got the molasses from the plantation mill in Hakalau. This was the fresh cooked topping for their meals. Served first and dry was pig meal bought commercially as a food supplement, much like vitamins are used in today's diets. The slop quenched thirst after the dry meal was consumed. This swill was fed twice a day and yielded hogs that were of good size and well finished. The results brought a contract for Lujan pork with Hilo meat markets.

He did all this with a 1938 Ford 8N tractor and a Massey Ferguson power take off system, a 9N Ford tractor, a Dodge power wagon with winch, and a 1948 Dodge truck. The tractors were equipped for ranch work as well as the heavy work in the cane operation. It takes three years to get a cane crop. It required planting, cultivating, and keeping grass out of the rows so that the grass did not end up consuming the fertilizer before the cane did. Originally cut by hand, Samuel Ho'olohekamohoali'i resorted to contracting with the plantation to cut the cane mechanically. Fleets of Kensworth trucks were replacing the droves of hand laborers across the cane fields of Hawai'i because the cost of mechanization was too much for an independent cane planter to bear individually. So he resorted to what in today's world would be called "outsourcing."

For all of his innovations in both ranching and cane planting, Samuel H'oolohekamohoali'i was awarded the first Outstanding Planner and Rancher of the Hamakua Coast Award by the state conservation district. He was also elected director of the Soil Conservation District Commission and held that post for thirteen years. He was touched by the Outstanding Planner and Rancher

Award and the State of Hawai'i Department of Natural Resources Certificate of Merit for his years as director, given to him at a special dinner in his honor at the Honoka'a Club. Not being a man of words, he humbly thanked the district officials and his 'ohana for his success and service. He kissed Alice and thanked his children with deep *aloha*.

The tension of change was becoming evident all across the Hamakua Coast. The 'ohana wanted a resting place for weekends and holidays, a place where time could pause to let their souls refresh. Since Lucas Lujan had passed in 1936, his house had been largely unused. So the Lujan house that had sheltered thirteen children and using education as their tool, their children would be used as the house of rest. Samuel Ho'olohekamohoali'i took it apart board by board. He found three adjacent house lots in the volcano and bought all three lots, one to be used right away and two kept for future use. The plan was that in the end, there would be one lot with a house and two available for the remaining two children when they had matured and were old enough to use the lots well. He rebuilt Lucas's house on one of the lots and left the other two free as a place for the children to play. He also added a fireplace to the house. For years, the Volcano House was the Lujans' *ho'onanea*, the 'ohana's place of rest.

The times spent at the volcano were enjoyed immensely. The sweets and candies at the Hongo Store still taste as they did in the memories of Sam and Alice's children. The tricycle rides as a youngster with my sister still live in vivid memory. Memories of the plums, thimbleberries and blackberries of summer still kindle the tastes of joy brought by the fruits of the volcano. For years, Leilani and I roamed through the architecture of stumps, fallen trees, and moss in the forests of the volcano.

Ho'onanea was located at twenty-nine miles from Hilo. You knew you were there when you arrived at Hongo Store. A stop there was mandatory to visit and to pick up groceries. The fireplace in the house was lit, and dinner by the fireplace was a romantic treat. The marines and army had a camp at the volcano used for rest and recuperation by the military. The officers' quarters were ample rather than luxurious. There was a movie theater on the base, and the residents of Volcano were allowed to use it. And the 'ohana did.

But the real adventure was the Hawai'i Volcanoes National Park. It was a short hike from Ho'onanea, and the hiking trails in the Volcanoes were wonderful. In addition to the sulfur springs, the berries, the young edible fern shoots, and the craters, there were over a hundred varieties of finches in the park. It was music to the ears and made a hike and lunch in the lava forest an outdoor concert, reminiscent of their wedding night.

It was also a time to gather herbs, especially the *'ohelo kaula'au*. Being so close to the park made it feel like it was the family's own playground. And a real treat was to eat at the Volcano House Restaurant. Sunday brunch was *'ono*, delicious. And visiting Aunty Tina Ignacio Short at the Keakealani School principal's house next door was always fun. Meanwhile, as the times were ticking away toward statehood, the 'ohana was schooling itself to adapt to the skills and professions of the new Hawai'i.

University of Washington commencement taken in 1985.
Leilani receiving her Ed.D from Vice President Herman D. Lujan

The Lujan women were leading the way using education as their tool. Alice had her master's, and she became the field assistant for speech and reading for the Big Island. No student attending public school did not know Mrs. Lujan. Leilani finished high school at St. Joseph High in Hilo and then went to Holy Names College in California getting her bachelor's degree. She then married her high school sweetheart, Albert Quiocho. He was an enlisted officer in the US Marines. She had four boys: Kevin, Kenneth, Keithan, and Kristian. She then got her teaching certificate and taught in the San Diego area. I married Carla Wayne Williams, adopting her two children, Laura and Mark. We also had one son, Timothy Samuel. With children to support, Carla did not complete high school but went directly to work. She would compensate for this later.

Like Alice, Leilani and Carla turned to education as the pathway to getting ahead. Leilani taught for the Santee School District. And like her mother, she went part-time to Azusa Pacific College to get her master's degree in education, which she did.

After she got her master's, Leilani decided to pursue her doctorate in education. She went to the University of Washington in Seattle, full time. She had those four boys and had to give them parenting as their father was always at war, and Vietnam was where he really lived. Like her mother, she was interested in teaching reading and speech to non-English speakers, the children of the immigrants. Alice focused on the immigrant cane workers. Leilani was focusing on the Latino and Asian language speakers. The world's leading scholar on this topic was at Washington and became her major professor. Sam Sebesta was the best there was, and he took Leilani on as a student. After her doctorate, she was completed her career in K-12 education as a teacher, district professional development coordinator in the Santee School District, elementary principal in San Bernardino County, middle school principal in Alpine Union School District, and director of professional development at the San Diego County Office of Education in North San Diego County. In 1996, Alice was hired as a professor at California State University, San Marcos. She coauthored a leading text on reading. She is under contract to do another related book.

Not to be outdone, Carla passed her general education examination (GED) after Timothy Samuel was born and was going to school. She enrolled at the University of Kansas, where I was a faculty member and administrator. She completed her Bachelor of

Social Work (BSW) at the University of Washington. She then enrolled in graduate studies and completed her Master of Social Work (MSW) at the University of Washington. Going from a high school sophomore dropout to an MSW at a leading university was no small feat. Carla completed her career as a professor of social work and directed the Bachelor of Social Work undergraduate program at California State University, Los Angeles.

I began becoming serious about education while attending St. Joseph High School in Hilo. I was a good student, and I worked hard, graduating as the class valedictorian. I also became interested in the priesthood, and my preference between them varied two and fro. When I mentioned the possibility to my parents, my mother—a devout Catholic—was awash in hope and joy. My father was pleased but cautious about the whole matter. After several conversations with the family, I decided to give it a try. Upon graduation from St. Joseph, I packed up in August 1953 for the trip to Kaneohe, Oahu, and St. Steven's Seminary.

The seminary was located on the Old Pali Road just north of Kailua, Oahu. It was nestled in between shrubs and trees, buffering the buildings from the highway and the outside world. The grounds were bucolic and bountiful in buds and the melodies of finch and squawking mynah birds. It was an easy place to be spiritual and reflective. It was a place where my dilemma could be solved.

The seminary was in the hands of the Sulpician Fathers, a Catholic religious order specializing in seminary work. The priests were skilled teachers, and they knew how to create community among the seminarians. They relied on meditation as a key tool along with introspection and personal advising.

I was the only high school graduate among them and therefore was the eldest of the thirty or so seminarians. I made friends with the older students. Because I had graduated, I took only those classes needed for transfer to the diocesan seminary at Palo Alto in California. This gave me one half day each day for myself to mull things over. I usually walked out to the athletic field to think things through and get a better sense of what would fit and what would not. After one year, armed with the advice of a father confessor along with a better sense of self, I left the seminary to my mother's sadness and my father's understanding.

Two stories reflect the changes I went through socially. The first involved my efforts to become an Eagle Scout. I performed all the requirements, and I was a Life Scout. All I needed was to pass a swimming test. Well, two things interfered. I was scared of water, and I was an asthmatic. So Frank Ferreira, my Eagle Scout buddy, convinced me I should go with him to the Boiling Pots ponds at the Rainbow Falls in Hilo. There, after some coaching, I launched off into the tepid water. Halfway across the pond at the foot of the falls, I began to fail—I could not breathe, and I panicked. Frank saw me. He immediately came to my rescue and saved my life. When it all sank in, I began to realize that life was not to be taken lightly.

The second story is in a lighter vein. It was prom night at St. Joseph High. The family drove to Ho'onanea in the volcano for the weekend. While there, they were going to paint the outside of the house. Frank Ferreira and I were double dating, since I had the car. I had just gotten my license, so this was a big deal. The dance went well, and we took the girls out for sodas and smooched by the Hilo Bay. I was to be at home by eleven, the dance ending at ten. But we let the time slip by. Being late, we rushed the girls home and then headed for Peleau. The exit road to Hamakua ran along the edge of Hilo Bay. A storm had brewed as we took the girls home. When we got to Mooheau Park, the waves were washing over the road and rising as each wave slapped the shore.

Then, as quick as a cough, a wave picked the car up and lifted it to the edge of the road. The car engine stopped cold. The waves grew in leaps and bounds, and we were stuck. The water was getting rougher. Frank wanted to scale the fence; I wanted to stay with the car. Fortunately, Frank won the argument. We scaled the fence and watched the car rock. The police saw this and came to where we were in the park. The officer let me have his phone, so I could call the manager of the Dodge dealership Mr. Botelho, who was my father's friend. He towed the car to the garage and gave me a loaner. We then headed home.

Well, the next day, we drove to the volcano. We got there late but just in time to watch a father lean away from the paint brush and begin the inquisition.

"How was the dance?"

"Fine."

"Have a good time?"

"Oh yeah!"

"What time did you get home?"

"Just a little late?"

"Is that so! Then explain this!" said Dad as he came down off the scaffold. There it was. Front page of the *Hilo Tribune-Herald* newspaper. A picture of the family car, floating on the frontage road and the reporter giving the time as after 1:00 a.m.! Punishment was on its way. Dad simply said, "Give me the keys." I was grounded for the next month.

Apart from being the class valedictorian, I had put together a group of friends whose ambitions paralleled mine. Clifford Rezentes, Frank Ferreira, Eldon Johnason, and Sam Pa were the "brotherhood" of high school friends I had. But the brotherhood had been put into hiatus when I decided late in my senior year to try the Catholic seminary to begin studies for the priesthood. I had thought of the priesthood off and on for some time; upon graduation in 1953, I went to the local St. Stephens diocesan seminary in Honolulu. As I mentioned earlier, I went; and after a year in seminary, I left, finding the regimen not always a good fit.

I applied for and received admission to Saint Mary's College in Moraga, California. I applied there because Clifford, Frank, and Eldon had all gone to Saint Mary's. A brother, Albert Rahill, personally recruited me, and the hometown brotherhood had extended itself to California. In California, my classmates dubbed me the "saltwater wetback" since Lujan was a Spanish name, and I was a "wetback" coming by way of the ocean. Nuances of race were something present in Hawai'i but not as engrained as I would come to learn they would be on the mainland.

The first reminder was the requirement that people from the Territory of Hawai'i had to report to federal government authorities once each year at the beginning of the calendar year. The person had to go to a US post office, as aliens did, to get the appropriate forms. I went to the college post office for the forms and filled in the required information. My full name was Herman Damien Leilehua Lujan. The postmaster told me that I could only have one middle name, and Leilehua would have to go. It was a "foreign" name. I argued for a while and in frustration went along with dropping my kanaka name. That act would stalk me for the rest of my life. The name given to a kanaka maoli was disallowed by a postal clerk. My sense of genuineness and true personage was being muted. It was the silence of hope one more time.

The second reminder involved a date to a college mixer. I had a date with a student from Belmont College, a Catholic private college for women in Palo Alto. When I picked her up, I was asked into the house where I was grilled about the background of my family and parents. And what was my culture. I answered the questions, with my date feeling increasingly uncomfortable. It was evident the family was not comfortable with me. And I was not comfortable with them either. The evening was awkward. And there were no more dates with the belle from Belmont.

Chapter Nine

Connections

Ho'ohui

I found places of joy and genuineness among the Saint Mary's brotherhood. Frank Urias, a Mexican American from Santa Paula near Oxnard, California; Mickey McKinna, Vince Varela, and Ben Castor also of Oxnard; Alf Collins of Lake Chabot, California; Ron Sceglio of Pomona, California; Mike Mase of Inglewood in Los Angeles; David Neitling from Stayton, Oregon; Darryl Gunther of Nevada; Joe Nargie of Los Angeles; Jerry Salac, a Filipino American from San Martin, south of San Jose, California; Libert O'Sullivan, a kanaka from Honolulu; and the Saint Joseph "brotherhood" from Hilo.

These relationships were lifelong. They included more than just friendship. They helped with personal issues, including study sessions; job referrals for those who were working their way through college; tutoring; personal support; a place of respite for those who could not go home for holidays; and just plain friendship. Frank

Urias was the first of this second brotherhood I met. Upon arriving on campus, he was the first person I saw and to whom I spoke. He helped me settle in and put me at ease. He picked lemons, and I began my working by doing hoe *hana* (weeding) in the sugarcane fields. From simple beginnings, we ended up in college and away from home.

Frank got to Saint Mary's through a scholarship from an elderly lady in Oxnard. I received a President's Scholarship to cover tuition and fees. Frank's benefactor found students with promise and paid their costs at Saint Mary's. His family was low income, and her generosity was deeply appreciated by Frank. Besides, this was a sure bet. Urias would not let her down. Frank went on to become a lawyer specializing in labor issues. He married Eva, the smartest thing he ever did. We stayed in touch, and had many barbeques which included two other Gaels, Saint Mary's students Ben Castor and Vince Varela. We solved all the world's problems and drank enough to increase the price of tequila at the local liquor store! Frank remains the philosopher among us and a wise one at that.

Alf Collins had a car and a way with words for which an Irishman would kill. He took on any topic and was quick in reply. He was the college newspaper sports editor, and he and I worked at the statistics table for basketball games; I typically got courtside seats to cover rebounds. Alf also sat courtside and handled all the other statistics. These were the days of Bill Russell at the University of San Francisco and Tom Meschery and Odell Johnson, our Saint Mary's basketball stars. The former went on and played and coached pro basketball. He retired and is a respected poet. He now lives in Sacramento. Odell became the president of Laney Community College in Oakland, California. He is retired.

Alf graduated and went to work at the *Turlock Journal*. After covering the marches at Selma, Alabama, Alf moved to Seattle and the *Seattle Times*. He covered real estate and then food. By now, I had arrived in Seattle, and our friendship was renewed. He did restaurant reviews, and I became a sidekick in sharing the cuisine. We found a favorite, Kaspar's Restaurant. As the kanakas would say, "The food was so good, it broke the mouth!" Translated, the food is so good that I do not want to eat again. Alf married Shirley, the original owner of Sur La Table, a culinary supply store. She was known by every respectable restaurant in Seattle. She finally sold it, and they both retired to Whidbey Island where they grow vegetables and seasonings and turn simple food into gourmet fare.

Ron Sceglio was the quiet one. A lawyer-to-be, he never put on the lawyer's persona. He looked upon practicing law as a helping profession and lawyers as people who connect the law with the "lawyered." We were roommates after graduation, and we both worked for an Italian restaurant in Berkeley, La Val's Pizzeria. We helped each other in the transition from college to a profession. Ron ended up in the army and was stationed in Texas. There he met his wife, Maria. She raised two lovely girls. When I moved to Southern California in 2001, we were able to get together regularly. And we did, until I moved to the Bay Area in Northern California. Cell phones, email, and occasional class reunions are the new vessels for nurturing friendships.

Mike Mase was one of my roommates at Saint Mary's. He was bright and cerebral. He knew his wines and foods and was always ready to pursue a good meal. His mom was the cook. She made the best tongue and cabbage this farm boy ever had.

Apart from good food, I could confide in him, and he always gave good advice. He had an abiding interest in European history, especially Italy. That became his major. When we were roommates, his interest in Hawai'i grew. He spend a summer in my home at Peleau. Peleau was no Waikiki. He learned about sugarcane, hogs, and cattle. We did the sightseeing on weekends and led the real life in between them. Mike got more than a suntan during that summer in Hawai'i. He got a taste of life in the 'ohana. Mike has been a professor of Italian and European history at Golden Gate College. We stay in touch even though he lives in Portland, Oregon.

Then there was Dave Neitling. The guy from Stayton, Oregon. His mom ran the local hardware store, and his dad ran around. Dave was gregarious—a person of unstoppable energy, an avid reader, and the source of well put but occasionally flawed arguments. He was very athletic, doing marathons into his seventies. But he balanced that physical feat with solid academic analysis. He became a banker after Saint Mary's and is now retired. We stay in touch. He usually calls, and we dissect the world around us. Each year, he sends us packaged Bing and Rainier cherries from his wife's, Juanita's, family farm. Juanita was a chemical engineer and lumber business executive until she retired.

Darryl Gunther was the godfather of the brotherhood. He was a retired navy veteran who was close with Dave Neitling and me. He lived off campus in a little trailer nestled among the pear trees of a nearby orchard. He left on weekends to work in Lake Tahoe as a cashier at the Crystal Bay Club Casino. He often took me with him. I would bus tables for one shift and shill for the house for the second shift. Along with another shill, we would start up games at empty tables. As soon as the action was going, we left for another vacant table.

I shilled for Blackjack. One evening, I went to an empty table to start the game. As the table began to build, my roll came around. I rolled a seven. Then an eleven, followed by another eleven. By now the table was teeming with bettors. The dealer was concerned. The pit boss, the person with oversight of a section of tables, was visibly uptight. I kept on rolling. I rolled eleven consecutive rolls of seven and eleven combinations. On the twelfth role, I rolled two craps. The dealer cleared the table and paid the winners. The pit boss came by, gave me a twenty-dollar bill, and told me to get my tips and get to the bar and cool off. I had lost the house $80,000! I pocketed my tips and headed to the bar for a 7 and 7, a 7 Up and Seagram's Seven Crown bourbon drink.

Then came Joe Nargie, everybody's jazz artiste. He played a mean piano and did for his whole life. But as the son of an ambitious Italian father, he needed to study something that paid and was "a real job." Joe decided on medical school. It only half filled the bill. Joe was the boy who needed to impress his father. But that was not to be. What was to be was a long trek through medical school at UCLA. He graduated and along the way met a young nurse, Pam. The rest is pure soap opera. They fell in love, and Dr. Nargie opened practice in Templeton, north of Paso Robles, California. He hung his shingle as a cardiologist and developed a solid practice.

We reconnected after I moved to Los Angeles and visited regularly until he passed. He had a unique talent at the jazz piano. He could roll those ivories until the midnight hour.

His persona would lighten up when he spoke of his grandchildren. When he retired, his concern was a legacy for his grandchildren. So he made hand-carved trains each year as Christmas presents. This talent for the human touch was his signature of life. From surgery to the grandchildren's toy box, Joe always delivered with the human touch.

Jerry Salac came from a family of Filipino farmers in San Martin, California. His family tended strawberries on the lush soil south of San Jose. He went home every weekend to help the family. He was quiet, reflective, and he had consummate patience. Occasionally, he would take many of us to his aunt's apartment in San Francisco near Natoma Street. These were occasions that always involved tasty Filipino delicacies. They also were places where the Filipinas in the family were present. The food was tasty to the palate. The girls were eye candy for the boys. Jerry should have been a diplomat, for he was the best communicator of the brotherhood.

Mickey McKinna was the Jimmy Dean of the brotherhood. He was strikingly handsome, a good conversationalist, and a lover of semi-trucks. As you might think, a guy with this range of talents was going to have to holster some of these attributes, so he could graduate. He roomed with Frank Urias and was going to need all the help he could get. So the brotherhood became the bullpen from which Mickey could get what he needed as tests came around. Career-wise, he went into the navy and retired as a naval officer. He had his own ship when he retired.

He turned to his second love—trucking. He is still in the truck driver training business in Federal Way, south of Seattle. He had a great family. I helped his son get into the Border Patrol. I also helped his daughter get into UCLA for a PhD in psychology. They are both successful in their career choices.

I was actively connected and involved in student endeavors at Saint Mary's. I was a student representative to the student council for all four years and was class president. I lost the student body presidency by one vote. I was notorious for having organized the first food strike over food quality and a monotonous menu. The strike lasted for a day until the president decided to work with the students to change things. The food was better and more varied after the strike. I graduated in 1958 receiving the Robert MacMillen Student Leadership Medal.

With help, my academic record got me into the University of California, Berkeley graduate school to study political science. My professor at Saint Mary's also taught at Berkeley and praised my work to the professors in the Berkeley department. This helped me get admitted.

Saint Mary's was a small school with a modest reputation. It was known for its Great Books Program in which students read all the great western philosophers as a requirement for graduation. So the connection to Berkeley on the part of my Saint Mary's professor, Victor Ferkiss, was a needed boost. The Berkeley campus was a top university worldwide in political science. And its students were from Harvard, Columbia, Princeton, Yale, Chicago, Wisconsin, and Indiana—the top universities nationally in political science. The burden of proof was totally on me.

Help came early. My first seminar was under the world's top expert in American politics, Dr. Peter Odegaard. He opened the seminar with questions about the nature of analysis and the use of logic. He then asked the class what the "square of opposition" was. Students responded but were all off target. I studied the term at Saint Mary's, so I addressed the question. It was a form of logic developed by Aristotle in his work on the nature of logic and logical inquiry. I learned that in the Great Books Program at Saint Mary's. My answer was spot on. Odegaard called me aside after class and said he would like to have me work with him on my thesis. Odegaard's schedule was cramped since he was offering a nationwide course on the American constitution and politics by television through NBC. So he was out of town in New York for two days a week, and other work flooded the rest of his schedule. Peter Odegaard told me that he was free after seminar if I was interested. On Tuesday nights, I could join him for a little dinner at his home and go over the seminar and the thesis. Personal tutoring on Tuesdays by the world's leading mind was not bad for the kid from Saint Mary's.

The consequence was a hellacious daily schedule for me. I was working as cook in a local pizza restaurant called La Val's. Monday was a day off from work and was therefore a day to study and write assignments. On weekdays, the schedule was class from eight to ten; lunch from ten to two; class from two to four; study from four to five; bartend from six to eight; and class from eight to ten. Then work from ten to 1:00 a.m. and close the restaurant. Carla was up when I got home and had dinner ready for me. We both retired and got up at 7:00 a.m. to get the children to nursery school. Carla then worked the day shift as a waitress. Graduate study at Berkeley was not for the weak or faint of heart.

In December 1959, Carla and I were wed. In June 1960, I went home to Peleau to help my father with the cane crop, diploma in hand and Carla with child. In September of 1960, I began teaching at St. Louis High School in Honolulu. It was kanaka Brother Oliver Aiu who convinced the brothers to hire me. And he tutored me from time to time.

The students at St. Louis High School were placed in homogenous classes based on test scores. The Stanford-Binet test scores were used for placement. I got the classes below the school average score. It was quickly evident that the lower scored students were hampered by less than average reading scores. And poor reading contributed to poor writing. I collected the textbooks and had students use them as reference materials. In American government, if the topic was studying the constitution, the class would read the constitution as the primary study material. In addition, each student had to read the document as homework to prepare for class discussions the next day. To address writing, each student would turn in a one-page synopsis of what they read. Classes were conducted as little seminar groups, so individual and group learning could occur. Writing improved noticeably, and the capacity to parse and analyze content also improved.

A good number of the students I had were from poor homes. It was not unusual to have the Honolulu police come to class to pick up one of the students. I gave these students personal attention to keep them up with the class.

After two years, I was leaving St. Louis for doctoral studies at the University of Idaho. In my last class, the students thanked me, and then they gave me a large bottle of Old Taylor whiskey. None were old enough to buy it, so I have my views about how they got the bottle. I have never been sure if the bourbon was stolen or not!

As for me, I applied to several universities. On advice from Peter Odegaard, I looked at universities in the west. At the same time, Congress was creating the National Defense Education Act (NDEA,) a four-year scholarship program. In 1962, the award was for $3,800 per year which was a fair sum of money, especially for those who were married with children. I packed the family, and with new baby Timothy in tow, the 'ohana left Honolulu and headed for Moscow, Idaho, the home of the University of Idaho.

I was one of five NDEA grantees from Idaho. Senator Frank Church from Idaho was head of the senate education committee and had been point person for the funding of this legislation. Most states had a handful of awards. Five was a lot for a state the size of Idaho. I was the first to arrive in Moscow and size up the faculty. Bernie Borning was department chair. H. Sidney Duncombe had just completed his degree at the University of Washington and took a liking to my work. The dean of the College of Arts and Sciences, Dean Martin of Stanford, wanted me to do my dissertation under him. But I felt I had to avoid a situation where I would be researching someone else's interests. That was a surefire recipe for failing to complete writing the dissertation. Alert to the issue, Robert Hosack intervened. He indicated to Martin that the best fit was with the new professor from the University of Washington. Duncombe kept me caught up and current in political science. Hosack thought and taught systemically, especially in comparative government and international relations. He arranged a one-on-one seminar with me each semester. The small department of five faculty took ownership of the kid from Berkeley, especially Professor Cliff Dobler, a scholar of constitutional law. He kept in touch with me until his passing.

Photo taken in Moscow, Idaho of Samuel, Herman and
Alice Lujan celebrationg Herman's Ph.D.

Samuel and Alice Lujan celebrating Herman's graduation.

In June 1964, I received my PhD from Idaho. Samuel Hoʻolohekamohoaliʻi and Alice were there glowing with pride. So too was Carla's mother, Louise Hill, and stepfather, Bill. The ʻohana had reached the pinnacle in education. Idaho had also produced its seventh PhD outside of forestry or geology. Idaho was broadening its degree offerings, and there were more students on their way. When I had to defend my thesis, the whole social science faculty attended the exam. It was a signature day for the political science faculty. It was a banner day for the ʻohana.

I left the ceremony with my degree and with a job at the University of Kansas (KU). Once more, connections helped pave the way. Kansas had a vacancy in American politics and in research methods. The chair of the Kansas Department of Political Science was Ethan Allen. He was calling around the country trying to find a hire for that slot. He had gotten nowhere. So he called Clara Penniman, the chair of political science at Wisconsin. She had no graduates who qualified. But her brother, also a political scientist, talked to one of his faculty who thought he knew of someone to fit the niche. That faculty member was Victor Ferkiss. Allen hired me, and I began my research and teaching. My family started to settle in when we began to see the other face of Lawrence, Kansas. The sight was not reassuring.

On the day we arrived in Lawrence, we had been on a long hot drive in early September. The children were exhausted and hungry; it was one o'clock, and the heat was in the low one hundreds. We saw a restaurant that was open and parked the car. As we entered the door, all eyes focused on us. A low mumbling followed, but no one moved to greet or seat us. Tim, our youngest, was crying as he had an infected ear and a fever that was not trivial. We needed water and a meal for the children. Mom, not one easy to intimidate, decided that we would seat ourselves. And we did. No one moved except to exit. Finally, the waitress came over and indicated that the restaurant was closed. Mother pointed to the sign on the door which read "Open." The waitress replied that the kitchen was closed anyway. Mother parried with letting us see the cold food menu. The cold salads and sandwiches were ample fare for a hungry family—a family that was not going to leave without being served.

The silence continued as people left. Finally, the cook intervened and told the waitress to take the order. She did, begrudgingly. She slammed the water glasses and stomped her feet into the kitchen. We sat for nearly two hours before we were served. And we took our time eating as we were trying to figure out what was behind the behavior we saw. Mom deduced that this was a racial incident. Dad was a dark-skinned Hawaiian, and he wore Wellington boots with gray khaki pants and a long sleeved shirt with a jade ornamented string tie. He looked Black or Native American. Since we were in Lawrence, Kansas, home of the Haskell Institute—a Native American junior college—Dad was taken to be Native American. Native Americans were not always welcomed in town.

The second shoe fell later in the day when we went to look at a rental home that was available. It was located right next to Haskell. The owner was a bit aloof, but he was not off-putting. He took to giving advice about the Haskell students. He told me that there was a curfew for them. It was 6:00 p.m. on weekdays and 10:00 p.m. on weekends. There was only one street into Haskell, so the students often used the backyard of the rental as their path to their dormitory. The hint was that we should lock the fence door in our backyard. The action was to keep this modern day Underground Railroad open. So we took the rental, and the gate was never locked.

The university treated me better. In three years, I was promoted to associate professor and elected chair of the KU political science department. I was also directing a million-dollar grant to study politics in Central America, an area of interest for the Ford Foundation. I led a program funded by Ford to take KU graduate students in political science or public administration to Central America. Six Kansans and six Guatemalans were selected. The Americans would speak and write in Spanish in the seminar, and the Central Americans would speak and write English. The focus was on the role of local governments and municipalities in public administration and economic development. The research project was very successful, and it led to my first published book. It was titled *La Administracion Publica Para El Desarollo en Guatemala*, and it focused on public administration and development in Guatemala.

The seminar was for a summer. I took my family and six KU students to Guatemala. The students lived with my family. My children adapted quickly to the local environment. Rather than live in the American district (Zone 10) as was the common practice among Americans, I leased a home in a middle-class Guatemalan neighborhood (Zone 7). All were expected to experience Guatemalan life by living among Guatemalans and being exposed to their culture. But living among them had its downside. You had to cross Guatemala City to *la Carretera Roosevelt* (Roosevelt Highway) to get home from downtown Guatemala City, passing through some of the most dangerous parts of the city.

On the Fourth of July, I invited several Peace Corps students for a barbecue. One of them needed a ride home to a location near the *barranca* (the city garbage dump). It was dark when I left to drive the young worker home, and it was raining very heavily. In addition, it was a habit of guerillas to steal foreign license plates from cars and use the plates as cover in their activities. By law, all *turistas* had to use *placas turistas* (tourist license plates).

Driving in the rain with low visibility, I took a wrong turn and ended up going the wrong way on a one-way street. Within minutes, an army truck came rushing around the corner. It stopped and out came the *ejercito* (army), guns at the ready. Good thing the Peace Corps student was fluent in Spanish (I was not). A soldier ordered the windows down and wanted to see my driver's license. I kept it in my grip just in case we had to make a run for it. After interrogation, the soldier finally stepped back, warning me to get out of the area. Bravery was not a useable attribute that night. I fled, dropped off the Peace Corps worker, and drove the long way home on the less dangerous periphery streets to return to *la Carretera Roosevelt*.

This was not the first brush with the Guatemalan army. On the way to Guatemala, we drove in two cars. I drove point. About an hour into Guatemala from Mexico, an army sergeant at the edge of a bridge waved the group to stop. Having army or immigration officials stationed at a bridge was not an uncommon practice. Since he was dressed as a soldier, we stopped. I ordered the group to stay in their cars and to keep the engines running. The more the guard spoke, the more he appeared to me to be an imposter. When he asked for my license, I told him to read it as I held on to it. The imposter kept saying it was not a license. It became clear in the exchange that the guard could not read. When he tried to grab the license, I yanked it back, rolled up the power window, tooted the horn, and hit the gas. The students followed suit. It was more than we expected to get in our pursuit of a taste of Guatemalan life.

Back at KU, I developed a group of graduate students who brought fresh ideas and backgrounds to graduate studies. It began with two students from Hawai'i, Michael Chun and Bina Mossman Chun.

Michael was studying public health, and Bina was in political science. She was pursuing a master's degree, and she needed a major professor to supervise her studies and the writing of her master's thesis. She and I talked several times, and I agreed to be her major professor. She was doing a thesis on voting patterns in Hawai'i, especially among Hawaii's ethnic groups. She wrote a superb thesis, which remains one of the early works on group voting patterns in Hawai'i. She spent her career in the University of Hawai'i Library.

Of the students that went to Guatemala, all completed their degrees except for Rick Mabbutt. He was a political theory student, and his insights were challenging and interesting. He was admitted to Harvard for graduate study and did not complete the degree. He returned to Idaho to be a university administrator and a community activist. He continues to work in the Latino health program area.

I discovered a promising international student in the course of teaching the required research methods class. He completed studies at the Ateneo de Manila in economics. He had been a student activist and was under pressure to leave the country. His life was in danger. He was Augusto Victor Ferreros. He was rigorously trained, especially in data analysis. He stood up intellectually to my challenges and completed his PhD under my supervision.

There were others of consequence at KU. One was a young Vietnam veteran, Ernie Garcia. He had run into Dr. Ken Martinez, the only Chicano professor at KU. Garcia was told by Martinez to visit with me. Ernie Garcia was bright but unfocused. He was not confident of his academic ability. He was selling shoes in a Wichita department store and was headed nowhere. He needed to go to college. I gave him a job working in the research institute I directed and got him enrolled. With his veteran benefits, he could afford college.

Ernie had a cousin, also back from the war. Steven Garcia walked into my office wearing an army jacket. He was articulate but apprehensive. This was a man who spared his words. What he said, he meant. While he was also a veteran with some benefits, he needed supplemental cash. The institute I directed needed a Xerox operator. Steve Garcia got the job and was on his way. The Garcias, who were cousins, had a third cousin, Sal Gomez. Sal was the dealmaker in the group. He was the quintessential entrepreneur, struggling with his classes while scavenging for a living. I got him some part-time work and nurtured him academically along with his cousins. He would graduate, but it would take time.

All of this was taking place while the Vietnam War was raging in the battlefield and across the country. Like other universities, Kent State was the spark that spread riot and contempt across the land. It even hit the streets of Lawrence, Kansas. The city responded with a curfew, bringing things to a head. The students had a leadership group who would not to talk to city officials. The city manager, a former student in the city management program in public administration, called me in along with law professor, Larry Velvel. We were the only persons with whom the leadership group would speak. At 10:00 p.m., as the curfew launched, the students pushed out onto the streets around the campus. The first police on the scene were the city police, who were considered quick triggers by the students. I met with the city manager privately. I urged City Manager Watson to let Velvel and me walk the streets on the campus boundary with the city and try to get the students off the streets. Watson agreed.

While I was patrolling on foot, a police car drove up, a rifle was shoved out of the open rear window, and I was ordered to approach the car and to keep my hands in sight. I protested that I was on the street with the city manager's permission and to please let me move the students at least on to the sidewalk. The city officer was not yielding and ordered me to get off the sidewalk, "Now!" Just then, another police car arrived with one of the ranking officers. He stopped everything and called the city manager who affirmed what I said. The patrolling helped. The students retreated to their residence porches. And all became quiet. I checked in with Watson, and I supported the view that the state highway patrol be called in as they were trained better for riot control. The city manager, the chancellor of the university, and the governor spoke. They agreed it was wise to make the change in night patrol across Lawrence.

The Vietnam War and the Cambodian incidents had another effect on KU. The effect was centered on the issue of the Reserve Officer Training Corps (ROTC). At KU, the program was small and the faculty few. The regular faculty was objecting to the lack of credentials among the military teachers. The courses were seen as sub-academic in the view of the general student body. The matter was rising on the agenda of the university senate, the body with jurisdiction on academic content in instruction. I was the chair of the university senate and was appointed by the chancellor and the senate executive committee to chair a senate committee on ROTC. I worked with faculty, student, military, and activist constituents to name a balanced committee, which we did. We had open hearings, and over a semester, we negotiated to common ground. The committee recommended that the courses had to be approved by normal KU procedures. The courses were to be listed as courses in history, credit would be authorized at that point, and the faculty had to be approved by the history department. This process of review spanned the fall semester and was going on as the decision on how the immediate course credit and graduation requirements would be met.

Given the general sense of crisis, exams were not held for the present semester, and students got the most recent grade earned in a course as the grade for that course. School ended after a university-wide meeting was held in the football stadium for a vote on this policy. The vote on the policy passed, and the crisis subsided until a young African American Lawrence resident was shot to death by the police on the campus near the student union building. It was too close to Kent State. The curfews returned as did the tension. With students gone, numbers were smaller, and violence diminished when cooler heads prevailed.

There were things on the lighter side in Kansas. When the state received a multimillion dollar federal grant to develop planning in the states, I was contacted by the governor's education policy assistant and the member of a small group of advisees assisting Democrat governor Robert Docking. Professor Mike Harder was a political scientist and was my colleague. Harder recommended me to the governor. The governor appointed me to be the first state planning director in Kansas. Its rank was equivalent to that of the Office of the Budget Director, Jim Bibb, who was considered the primary insider Harder wanted to buffer some of that influence and power. Appointing a state planning director gave a window for policy review, comment, and advice from Harder and me. I had one year to startup the office and help hire a permanent director. But the November election intervened. A Republican was elected governor, former state senator Bob Bennett. While Harder and I had free hands under Democrat Docking, things were going to change.

It happened that the chief of staff for Kansas senator Jim Pearson, Ed Flentje, was a Republican political scientist and a former student of mine at KU. Bennett, of course, knew Pearson. Flentje had left Pearson for staffing the Illinois State Board of Regents. In Flentje,

Bennett had a Republican staff aide to a Republican senator and someone who knew planning and research from his work with the Illinois State Board of Regents. The fit was there. If Bennett would okay it, the office's influence would increase under Flentje. Bennett approved, and Flentje was hired. Flentje, of course, needed a staff, and he had little experience there. So Flentje turned to me.

Flentje needed an assistant director and two staffers to start with. Well, I knew that Vic Ferreros, my PhD student at KU, was interested in research and planning. It also happened that the Office of Legislative Planning and Research in Kansas reported to a director who was by law a professor of political science at the University of Kansas. By law, the legislative research office was to be nonpartisan. When I was chair of political science and then as co-faculty of the seminar team taught by Harder and me, we had connections at the level of legislative research. Those connections would have state planning and the Legislative Office of Planning and Research as pragmatic partners rather than partisan opponents. Besides, Flente and Vic Ferreros were classmates under me. The fit was there. I had two other students looking for work in state government. Steve Garcia and Sal Gomez were skilled as students in planning. They knew Flentje from his PhD days at KU. In short, Flentje now had a team. It was a natural fit.

I taught American government at KU, and each semester, I would invite then-congressman Bob Dole to give a lecture on how congress worked. Dole had summer internships available in his office, and he wanted to know if I had any students for this opportunity. Ernie Garcia was available, so I sent Ernie to work for Dole. He started opening the mail and processing it and ended doing responses to constituents in Dole's district. When Ernie graduated, Bob Dole became senator. He made Ernie the director of his state field office in Topeka. So it was that Ernie became one of Dole's key staff.

When Reagan was elected president, Reagan named Elizabeth Dole the head of his transition team. This was the behind-the-scenes group that coordinated the hiring and releasing of executive employees. She needed a chief of staff. Bob Dole reminded her of Ernie, and Ernie was appointed to the team. His prestige and competency was rising quickly.

In the aftermath of the election, Bob Dole was elected Majority leader of the Senate. It is the top job in the Senate. The Office of the Sergeant-at-Arms was in play as the incumbent was leaving. Bob Dole immediately called Ernie Garcia to let Ernie know that Dole was nominating him for the job. A few days later, Ernie was named sergeant-at-arms. Few noticed, but he was the first minority sergeant-at-arms in Senate history and the first Mexican American in that job. Bob Dole was making history with the kids from Kansas. Ernie's influence blossomed in his appointment to the staff of the Secretary of Defense, Cap Weinberger. His role was as chief lobbyist for the department. He was the legislative mind behind Weinberger. Ernie was also still serving in the US Marine Corps Reserve. He had experience where Weinberger did not. Weinberger and he were a good fit. The secretary was a savvy strategist and made Garcia a key asset. Garcia put another notch in his handle of experience.

Back in Kansas, ethnic minorities were becoming more active. This was, after all, the state of Brown vs. the Board of Education. In the Mexican-American communities in Wichita, Topeka, Kansas City, Garden City, and other towns across the state, Mexican Americans wanted recognition. They coalesced behind establishing a Mexican American commission to provide access at state government offices and services. The legislation passed. Governor Docking needed a chair for the commission who could find common ground. I had advised him on community matters from time to time. He decided after consulting with Mexican-American leaders he knew, and my name came up in those discussions. First Mike Harder called about it. Then the governor asked to see me. After reassurances that the commission would have access at the highest level, I accepted the appointment. The commission met regularly, its budget was honored, and it went across the state, moving its meetings to where the Mexican-American communities were. The commission being operable, I left it.

Minority issues were also bubbling on the campus. It happened over a new course added to the political science course offerings. After discussions with African American students and the few African American faculty at KU we had, the course would be entitled Black Revolutionary Thought, and it would review the growing literature in the civil rights field. As chair of the department, I would host the course. The local state legislator from Lawrence—where the university was—read about the course in the newspaper the *Lawrence Journal World*. Locals went ballistic. Teaching revolution? They contacted the chancellor who talked to the provost Francis Heller. They were after my neck. Fortunately, the provost was a scholar, and he defended the right of faculty to teach both that which we like and that which we oppose. It did not help that I was team teaching the course with a local Black activist named Leonard Harrison. He was a "revolutionary" in the eyes of many locals. During my visit with the provost, I suggested that we rename the course Black Political Ideology and focus on Black political thought in general, and not on revolution. The provost checked around and met with some regents in private session. The name change assuaged the regents, but if they had their druthers, I would likely have been gone. There was one foot note to it all. I got a few focused words from the provost whispered in my ear and then learned the clincher. Leonard Harrison could teach, but I had to be there when he did. And Harrison would be paid by personal check from me. I would get a private check from the provost to reimburse me. No state funds were ever to touch Harrison's hands.

As you can see, I also had a professional life as a political scientist, a faculty member, and as the director of the Institute for Social and Environmental Studies (ISES). I administered the State Growth Policy Program for the state. This took me to visit most of the 104 counties and 386 cities in Kansas, especially during my term as state planning director. The regional planning districts also kept me on the road. Through ISES, I had access to planning students who actually did the planning for the small cities and counties. It was much needed technical assistance and kept rural Kansas competitive in the battle for jobs and economic development. I taught courses and made trips across the counties and state planning regions, urging a more strategic use of planning especially in critical policy areas such as water, housing, and the rural economy. These were areas where the problems were profound. For example, in water policy, wells were running dry before the pumping equipment was even being paid off. The problem was most critical in the Ogallala basin of western Kansas, and it remains a policy concern for Kansans.

I had a breadth of knowledge about state politics that was increasingly valuable. I got a phone call from the manager of NBC TV channel 27 KTSB, Topeka. He wanted in-depth color coverage of the elections. Legislators, governor's staff, and Mike Harder (he had a similar role for ABC News in Kansas City) had all suggested me. After my conditions were met, I agreed to serve. My role was to comment and provide predictions. The station's computer would feed me whatever I needed. I had a set of predictor precincts that I used that had always voted for the winner. I used my doctoral dissertation for the formulae to get the predictions. The regular evening news anchor was my partner.

It was the 1975 election. I was on from 6:00 p.m. to midnight when we called the winner. I had prepared maps to use as filler when results were not coming in. The manager liked the color analysis and visual aids I used along with my comments and verbal analysis throughout the evening. He was impressed enough to raise the possibility of my doing color commentary on KTSB opposite Paul Harvey, on the evening news at six and ten. I would tape once each week. I agreed and did the commentary until I left Kansas.

Ernie was not in office as sergeant-at-arms for very long when he noticed that senators were asking for money, each to have their own minicomputer. Minicomputers were the rage then. The cost was $26 million. Ernie needed help. He called me for advice. I had been one of the early users of computers at KU, and Ernie knew that. He asked if I would be agreeable to a contract to review the US Senate computer center. I agreed but only if Vic Ferreros could be part of the team. Vic had worked out very well as assistant director for planning research. But other additional elections came along, and Vic left to become the director of data information systems for the State of Alaska.

I called Victor, and we discussed the opportunity. This was high-level policy stuff, and all of us would gain if we did a good job. Ernie would give us broad discretion, and we needed that. Vic had direct access to Senator Ted Stevens who had seniority and an interest in data systems. Ernie had direct access to the new Majority leader, Bob Dole. And most importantly, Ernie had been named legislative liaison to Congress for the defense department and was chief lobbyist for Secretary of Defense Cap Weinberger. All of these connections meant good chances for leadership support.

This was a brainer project and a no-brainer decision. I took the consulting job. Vic flew to Seattle to meet me (my having become the vice president for minority affairs at the University of Washington). My UW position gave me some familiarity with Senator "Scoop" Jackson, a defense hawk; Congressman Norm Dicks, who was also a defense hawk; my congressman, Congressman Jim McDermott of Seattle; and House Speaker Foley of Spokane. Vic brought along one of his staffers from Alaska who had working knowledge of how Senator Ted Stevens of Alaska operated. The point being made here is that key legislators and their staffs are the gatekeepers. They could kill a project in a flash or rescue it from the trash bin. We had ample access to receive any proposals we might make. Our lead contact would be Senator Ted Stevens through our staff person who worked with Stevens in Alaska and Vic Ferreros.

We had Ernie set up the appointments with key legislators, the vendors who were busy lobbying for their product, legislative staff, executive branch staff, and the computer center staff. Several items surfaced from our interviews and research. The lobbyists had really done their work with staff and legislators about data processing. They had made the case for customized work for senators and related it to the need for security. They wanted their own staff doing research. The resistance to change was engrained, and people wanted everything as it was. We assessed the technical capacity of the center staff. On the whole, their skills were becoming dated and behind of the current trends in data analysis and management information systems (MIS) processing.

The sitting senate computer center director was technically dated in what she knew, and she wanted to keep her job. Her strategy was to hold off change, go with the every senator having a minicomputer. And do the same with the senate committee staff. The plan would have the computer center provide technical backup. The strategy was long-term in nature, and everyone knew that technology was changing faster than it took to pay for it. The team decided to keep that reality as the anchor of the proposed solution.

The complication was the fact that senate committees had staff. Some staff had seniority over their senators and were very powerful. So the vendors had the staff pushing their agenda. We would make the following case. Cost was the ceiling for options. To provide every senator and every senate committee with minicomputers was financially prohibitive. It also was a dated solution. Technology companies were doing research and building increasing capacity while shrinking size. Prime minicomputers were a step in that direction. Their solution was unwieldy and too costly. We recommended instead, that the senate leadership look at a centralized system in which a large mainframe would provide the hardware for the whole senate and its committees. Software could be used to customize needed solutions where a main frame was not applicable. The cost of centralization (one main frame) was less than the decentralized solution's cost. We also recommended the removal of the incumbent director to a role elsewhere and urged finding a new director. After discussions with the Majority leader Bob Dole, Secretary of Defense Cap Weinberger, and Senator Ted Stevens of Alaska, Ernie offered the job to Vic. One more time, connections brought opportunity. But once the opportunity was taken, capacity and expertise were put to work. Vic held the job for about seven years, even after Ernie left due to a change of political parties. I will return to Vic again in a few years. But let us not get ahead of ourselves.

Chapter Ten

The Influencers

Na Koikoi

As the pages of life unfold, we come to find the people and things that touched us in ways that helped us define ourselves. To *haoles* it is soul; to kanakas it is *mana*. *Mana* is the inner self, the person we turn into through the cumulative choices we make in life. And I made my share of them both good and bad. I was most affected in my life choices by my father, Samuel Ho'olohekamohoali'i Lucas Lujan and to some degree by Kupuna Abraham Pi'ianai'a, especially while he was head of Hawaiian studies at the University of Hawai'i, Manoa. My kanaka elders died young so that by the 1940s, when I was in my impressionable years, my kanaka uncles were gone as was the kupuna generation. I was left with my father and Grandaunt Tutu Maea, whom I rarely saw.

My father taught more by example than by didactics. He focused a lot on inner values, one of which is *ukupau*, "work before you get your rewards." It is a widely held saying among kanakas. Another is *lokomaikai*, "Be generous, gracious, and of a good disposition." Also widely used is "Eat what is put before you, for someday it may not come." These sayings required thought about their true meaning in a person's life. They are lived out by us as we mature. I like to think that the lacing together of these sayings is how we weave our sense of person, our mana, our tapestry of life.

Take the saying to "eat what is set before you." At our house, sayings like this were translated into expected behaviors. The customs and etiquettes at the dinner table led to expectations and manners set by our parents. At our house, you were expected to eat the dinner that was set. No one left the table until father did. The family would wait until that occurred and people excused themselves as they were leaving and returning.

Dinner was more than about food. It was also about *ukupau*, a reward for the day's work. So father had us go around the table one by one, giving the high lights of the day. Father would often ask, "And what did you learn from that?" He did this with both good and bad stories of the day. For him, these were learnings in both cases. As you can see, dinner was also the vessel of social discourse, telling stories and learning the life defining values, norms, and behavior. Mother, ever the speech teacher, forbade pidgin during dinner's discourse. If you wanted *poi*, you had to ask for it in the Queen's English.

Waste, *'uha'uha*, was another rule of life. Wasting food was especially unacceptable. At our house, you were expected to clean your plate, you were also expected to eat at least one bite of everything that was served. We learned to take smaller portions and consume them. I hated Chinese bitter squash stuffed with pork hash, and tomatoes. I also tried the "excuse me, but I need to go to the bathroom" routine. Spitting unwanted food down the toilet was too obvious, and it did not work anyway. Instead, I learned to swallow one or two bites.

Smaller portions of squash combined with the one bite rule solved my problem.

Then I found out that Dad had a heart after all. He recalled that dog was served at a dinner he went to when he was ten or so. Dog was a food relished by many kanakas, but it was foreign to my father's palate. Faced with a dilemma, he used the small portion rule and got by.

Respect (*mahalo*) was another rule of life. People, animals, and things deserve respect. All things deserved recognition for their role in our lives. Wood gave us canoes. Water gave wood life. People gave purpose to these elements. So when people took the canoe fishing, by throwing the small and young fish back into the water, they gave respect to the species in the form of a future life to maturity. Kupuna and the family *makua* all warranted respect. You listened to what they said because they had experience-based instincts and wisdom.

Being kanaka was more than just looking like a kanaka and fitting the Harry Owens "Princess Pupule" stereotype of the eye candy hula girl. And being kanaka was not the "Pearly Shells" of the Waikiki night club circuit either.

In 1981, there was a conference at the University of Washington on what it means to be kanaka. Kupuna Pi'ianai'a, Winona Rubin, and Gard Kealoha gave their presentations, and then a taping was made on the topic "Is Hawaiian a Race?" The taped interviewees were Pete Tabali, Pila Laronal, Sheila Manus Vootman, and me. Tabali and Laronal were professionals. Voortman was a vice president for community relations of a leading Seattle corporation, and I was at the time vice president for minority affairs at the University of Washington. We were careful in our conversation to make it clear that we were not speaking for all kanaka professionals. What I present here is the core of our effort to address not just being kanaka, but also growing your mana both personal and professional at the same time.

You cannot control your circumstances, but you can control your responses to them. The central circumstance for kanakas is that we live in an in-between world. There is the world of our mana and the world of professionalism. The latter is the world of individualism, competition, conflict, and hierarchy. It rewards conflict, thrives on self-confidence, and lauds self-promotion. It is all about self.

By contrast, kanakas are ʻohana oriented. We choose collaboration and *huis* (groups) over individualism and conflict. As the dominant value in conflict, we seek solutions and common ground over winning. While others learn by deconstruction and breaking things apart as the road to understanding, kanakas look for connections and commonalities and evidence from a holistic perspective of best practice and what will work. Kanaka professionals survive by navigating between these realities. That culminates in being quietly competent. It relies on identifying what the professional perspective accepts as "the way" or "the answer." Then overlaying what your mana suggests will make a fit or be a pathway to resolution. For kanakas, the anchor points are personal competency and mastery of the problem at hand.

My father always used to say, "Empty barrels make the most noise." By that, he meant let your competence speak for you in the behavioral world. In the world of values or ideas, always include your mana, as it helps you shape your professional responses. This way, your mana grows as you grow, both as a person and as a professional.

Empty barrels self-promote. The louder they get, the less they have in them. Kanakas do not put things in neon lights; we see modesty as a driving personal ethic and competency as the professional norm and not pushiness, nerviness, and self-adulation (*mahaʻoi*) as selfish and brazen. There is also a tendency to see modesty as the partner of passiveness. So among some kanakas, there is often the urge to ask permission of others before acting. Kanakas need to be comfortable in their choices and act in a timely way.

Speaking of time, kanakas do not keep *haole* time. One reason is that kanakas approach problem solving within a tradition of letting issues unfold in their own time. We ponder over issues. By doing this, we give room for new elements that might reframe the issues in ways that could open new pathways that have their own time and place. And keeping a balance among them is one of the challenges to resolution. But there is a problem that goes along with pondering. It can be confused with being indecisive. While kanakas develop a sense that everything in life has a fit, the challenge is to find it and implement it.

President Barack Obama exemplifies the attribute of pondering. He was schooled in Hawai'i and was exposed to the practice of pondering. As president, he has put off action on a particular bill. For example, he was heavily criticized for dragging his feet on the issue of same-sex marriage. Congress was pushing the issue of same-sex marriage as an example of indecisiveness and lack of presidential leadership. Obama's "evolving" as kanaka, "pondering," taking the time to look for the solution that fit the situation. The president—facing a very tough political decision—put off any action, arguing that he had not made up his mind. While the opposition was crying out for leadership from him, Obama was revealing a bit of kanaka pondering as he built his way toward resolution. When he finally decided, he came down on the side of allowing same-sex marriage.

Pondering also has found a place in Obama's foreign policy decision making. Take the case of the use of chemical warfare in Syria. The country was widely split over US intervention in the incident or not. Polls showed at least a 50/50 split. Polls on Obama's personal leadership showed him in the 30 percent bracket. He insisted on negotiating for weeks, holding several conferences with legislators, foreign leaders, key staff, and others involved in decision making. The president was widely criticized for being undecided. As you might expect, pondering was seen as indecision, wishy-washy and weak-kneed. He paid a price over the incident, and his leadership was muddled and hung in the balance of negotiation. While some saw him as wise, many were ready to baptize him as the conveyer of vacillation. The lesson learned here is that while pondering contributes to a decision, there are no guarantees of success in its use.

Pondering is also evident in Obama's foreign policy as exemplified by the slow use of diplomacy in the cases of Syria and the Ukraine. Using diplomatic deliberation rather than military action, the United States is avoiding further use of military forces by pulling US troops from Afghanistan and avoiding another war, a response supported by the broader American public.

My father always made the point that pondering works best when accompanied by competency and respect for all. He underscored the role of competency, especially the kind of competency that empowers others in your personal relationships through giving and living with respect for all. He taught me to "make the circle larger." Share what you learn and know and enable others to grow through that sharing. This sense of sharing to empower was to him the core value of being kanaka. Before you share, you listen and take stock of what the issues and facts are. You must ponder over the outcomes. Then you can act as a leader should. This perspective reflects his inoa *Ho'olohekamohoali'i*, which means "to listen and act as a leader should."

Speaking of leadership, Abe Pi'ianai'a and I met at the conference on Hawaiian culture at the University of Washington mentioned earlier. He was a guest participant and was very well known in Hawai'i. He had an enchanted life. He was an academic and was chair of Hawaiian studies at the University of Hawai'i, Manoa. In his younger years, he was captain of a Matson Lines ship. Before that, he also was one of the select kanaka youths participating in a survival experiment on Baker and Howland islands atolls in the Pacific. The experiment was a project under the US Department of the Interior designed to determine how one could live nominally on small islands and atolls in the South Pacific by living off the sparse land. The islands were also designed to function as weather stations to serve the vast seas of Polynesia.

The colonists lived in huts; fish was their staple, birds were ample, and seaweed was plentiful. They set flight paths for air planes. They kept weather logs and maintained journals along the way. Resupplies occurred every three months including food and water. These barren islands haven no fresh water, so it was used sparingly.

The war was proving to be a real threat. So on February 9, 1942, the last of the kanaka colonists was extracted, and the project came to an end. In 1954, two bodies were removed for burial back in Hawai'i at a veterans cemetery. Abe had learned the lessons of life, lessons he could pass on when he felt they were fitting.

On the academic side of things, Abe was interested in finding a place for advanced studies at the UH. He wanted a program for kanakas generally, but also one that could adapt to those who were gifted and talented. There was one such student in particular, a young chanter and student of ethnomusicology, Kalena Silva. I agreed to look into the situation and fortunately was able to get Silva admitted to PhD studies at the University of Washington. He studied under a world-class scholar at the UW, Dr. Robert Garfias. Dr. Silva is now on the faculty at the University of Hawai'i, Hilo.

On the matter of core values, Abe became a mentor to me and offered advice and thoughts that let me rekindle my sense of culture and mana. We had extended conversations for more than twenty-five years. We touched upon the rebirth of the culture, especially the return of the language in schools, the more accurate review of place names across Hawai'i, and concerns over the need for educating many kanaka professionals for the future of Hawai'i, especially in the age of technology. We spent many a night at Abe's favorite Chinese restaurant on River Street. We focused on how to fit the *haole* core values and their emphasis on individualism and the kanaka emphasis on 'ohana, sharing, respect even toward adversaries, and the need to make things right. *Ho'opono* is the term symbolizing this driving virtue. It has stuck in my head since then. Being a kanaka, I have a moral responsibility to be righteous both as a person and as a professional.

My reflections of the many conversations I had with him about being kanaka follow. We begin with presenting the two anchor points of kanaka culture, 'ohana and ho'oponopono. These are presented as direct quotes from his presentation at the University of Washington conference referenced earlier.

> "In ho'oponopono, it is usually required that all blood members attend or be part of the ho'oponopono process. There are times when some members of the family cannot be present. For example, in my own family, when my second son is at sea and has to spend a couple of months away from home, he cannot attend a ho'oponopono whenever we have one. So in absentia we think of him, and when he returns, a full report is made to him.

"Ho'oponopono has to be 'chaired' by a senior person in the family. This is desirable because the senior person in the family is considered to have wisdom. Usually, it is one of the elders in the family—whether it be male or female—would conduct ho'oponopono. The person who becomes the chair or leader of the ho'oponopono always opens the session by asking for guidance of the Christian God. This is all right. You have to have faith in something. But before that time, guidance was usually asked not of the great gods of Kane, Ku, Lono, and Kanaloa, but of the 'aumakua of the family. *Aumakua* as used here really has two specific and different meanings. An 'aumakua as the shark or as an owl is in anthropological terms a totem. But in Hawai'i, you also had the *'aumakua* which was the spirit of the departed person, usually the spirit of the elderly departed who were regarded to still be part of the family and with whom you conversed in spirit. So these spirits were the ones that the prayers were directed at for help, relief, and for *wehewehe*, which is definition and meaning.

"Now the first thing that happens is an asking, a *noi' i* (seeking knowledge and definition in detail), for guidance in conducting the ho'oponopono. The next thing the leader of the ho'oponopono does is state the problem. Now it may be that some members of the family do not know the entire problem, and this could be a problem in itself. So when the whole problem is laid on the table in its detail, and everybody knows what the problem is, then the major actors are given their day in court.

"In this process of giving testimony and explaining their feelings, there may be fights between brothers and sisters. They may start blaming each other across the table. The leader of the ho'oponopono will stop that immediately and say, 'If you have anything to say, you say it to me! If you others have any gripes, you wait until your turn comes, and then you may express them. But you do not argue with this person. You just talk to me.' In doing this, the leader cuts out all of the rubble and interference which, rather than serving to uncover facts, hides the facts amidst the exchange of loud voices. So the leader as referee, if you please, is in the position to conduct this ho'oponopono as it should be, a discussion focusing on the problem itself..."

"In ho'oponopono, there is a built-in effort to keep all focused on the problem at hand until you reach the stage when one says, 'You know, *hewa wau*, I am at fault. I am wrong.' At this point, you have arrived at the beginning of the solution. The minute one of the persons who is deeply engrossed in the discussion says, 'You know, I'm wrong,' you have the problem half solved. The other half of the solution has to come from the person who was wronged. That person must—particularly in a family meeting—say, 'I accept your admission, and I forgive you.' Now if that person does not say that, the problem is not solved. The reason for that is if a person is big enough to finally say, 'I am wrong,' then the person who was wronged must also be big enough to say, 'I accept the fact that you admit you are wrong, and now we can start on even terms.' This is the basis of ho'oponopono—the mutual recognition of the wrong and mutual forgiveness to allow for a fresh start and making amends.

"The whole process is brought to an end by sealing it with a closing prayer, a *pa'a*, a tying together of the whole family into a newly empowered family.

"Ho'oponopono and 'ohana are the twin pillars of the kanaka way of life. The former deals with setting things right and the latter with the family as the basic social structure. The family acts through the ho'oponopono tradition of making things right. 'Ohana is the gathering of the blood members of the family, including the adopted members in the family to bring their mana together and address issues affecting the 'ohana."

The main tool of the 'ohana is its mana, the inner power of each person's being and the special talents attached thereto. Elders teach that everything has mana, and the pooling of mana is the pathway to a gracious way of living.

These tools must be passed on as the generations pass by, or the 'ohana will decline. Education is the key antidote. In the past, when *hanai* (adoption) and *luhi* (to raise a child with loving care) were practiced, the passing of knowledge between generations was immediate and direct, typically taught by the kupuna (grandparents). But the family life of present times has diminished these practices, so the challenge for the 'ohana is to find other educational channels for passing on the wisdom and knowledge of times past. Of particular concern is the pace of information in the technology-dependent world of the present is of particular concern to everyone. Things like grades and other educational markers are in decline across the country. While math and science scores drop, dropouts grow, and teachers have challenges that test their traditional tools for learning to the limit. Non-kanakas push their offspring to the margin, ignoring their capacity to perform. Kanakas have the view that children should be taught when they are ready. There is a time and place for everything—that is the basic concept for learning. Youth will respond when they are ready, and teachers and *makua* (parents) need to ease off in the frantic search for performance. Aim high but be patient.

Students need a supportive environment in which to learn, and they need flexibility to set a pace that fits their pathway to learning. Most of the vignettes in this memoir reflect this. Support is manifest by supportive programs like the Office of Minority Affairs at the University of Washington. OMA built faculty support for English and math courses in particular. A study skills center offered course assistance and focused on group learning and used peer tutors. The OMA Early Identification Program served as a lever to encourage the promising students with an early start at the learning practices characteristic of graduate study. The course was taught by the UW "star" faculty. Serving the best with the best could only have excellent results.

The University of Washington became a hothouse for learning. It created a learning culture where the access to excellence was there for everyone. Some of the best minds among the faculty taught and exposed the students to the highest levels of excellence. Nobel laureates lectured to OMA and undergraduate students. Faculty shared how they got interested in learning their specialty of choice. The alliance between students and key faculty was the anchor point of their success.

Learning communities do not just happen. They are built course by course, person by person, and action by action. These relationships become a way of thinking and a way of living academically. Weakness and ignorance can be trumped by practice and the necessary infrastructure for learning excellence. In the end, it involves money.

The UW leadership saw this as an investment rather than a cost. Well-funded, the program persists and OMA students continue to exceed expectations.

It is especially touching to have minority students who were from OMA or in graduate studies at the UW move into the queue of for sustaining a supportive environment and to pass these practices on. Two come to mind. The present vice president for minority affairs Dr. Sheila Edwards Lang at the UW was my protégé. She completed her PhD and continues to find creative ways to help minority students exceed their expectations.

The second student was James Ortez. He also served as my assistant in undergraduate studies and also completed his PhD. He is presently assistant dean at the School of Social Sciences, Humanities and Arts, at the University of California, Merced. He has developed and put in place supportive services activities and programs, building them into the newest UC campus infrastructure.

While all of this was taking place, I was becoming increasingly interested in helping kanaka students get into the UW. I was a co-chair of the Hawai'i Leaders National Panel of the Administration Needs Assessment Study of 1979–1981 which was a project of the Administration of Native Americans (ANA) under the auspices of the National Institute for Mental Health (NIMH) of the federal government. This program was part of a larger needs assessment of Native American Indian needs. Through the panel, I came to know kanakas who were leading change in Hawaiian affairs back in Hawai'i.

As mentioned earlier, I also sponsored a Hawaiian Awareness Conference at the University of Washington. The visit to the University of Washington of Gard Kealoha (OHA), Winona Rubin (Alulike), Abe Pi'ianai'a (University of Hawai'i, Hawaiian Studies), and Ho'oulu

Cambra (the Kamehameha School), among others, was unique for the mainland where many kanakas live. This group of respected kupuna brought legitimacy to what we were doing. Winona Rubin's presence at the University of Washington was significant in the eyes of the kanakas in exile. There were more kanakas in exile on the mainland than there were at home, and the visit brought the 'aina and the 'ohana to them, and that symbolism was important to the mainland kanakas.

When the national panel went to Honolulu, I was privileged to meet for the first time with key kupuna Gladys Brandt and Frenchy De Soto. Both Winona Rubin and Gard Kealoha were there and helped frame the issues for the panel. In this way, we were able to identify the needs that seemed to fit the broad expectations of kanakas. A report went forward. While there were some actions taken, no major consequences emerged. What did emerge was increased visibility for legislation affecting kanakas and the active monitoring of these by the congressional delegation, especially the staffs of the Hawai'i legislators in Congress, Senator Dan Inouye and Senator Akaka.

Photo of Herman Lujan meeting with George H.W. Bush in his White House office in D.C.

On the professional side of things, a key figure in my development and savvy was William P. Gerberding, president of the University of Washington, now retired. When he arrived at UW, I was one of the carryover administrators from the previous president's regime. I was the vice president for the Office of Minority Affairs (OMA) at UW. That program served American minority groups at a time when special admissions for minorities was a wedge issue that split the country. It divided Americans and was especially problematic for minority administrators everywhere. These were few in number and were not producing graduates to meet the demand for them. In addition, many in public education felt strongly that grades alone should determine admission. With minorities scoring low on this criterion, the problem at Washington was worse. It was addressed at UW through the Office of Minority Affairs special admission program. Graduation rates were unacceptably low, so I began a program to send the unprepared to the community colleges and have them remediate there. If they did that, OMA would have the university admit them, and the students had to be responsible for using OMA's study skills resources to meet or exceed their current needs and university requirements.

The local minority groups saw this as a "creaming" program, where we would only admit the top students, and that meant a turning of our backs to the inadequacies of the neediest. Student and community groups united to pressure me and Bill Gerberding. They burned me in effigy at a rally of over four hundred students. Police were called in, and there were arrests. I received threatening phone calls at all hours of the night. The university police instructed me to arrive on campus by a different route each day. They would intercept me and escort me to a different parking space. Then they would drive me to my office. It was not a good beginning for the new president

Bill Gerberding. Despite heavy pressure, he refused to fire me and in fact quietly moved to see how the university could chart a course that would better link UW to minority communities. Senior minority faculty, minority alumni, and others helped carry the message on and off the campus. The policy offered was that those with low grade point averages would go to the community colleges and transfer back once remediated. The community colleges liked this for it asked them to do what they are good at—remediation. The program had good results as grades improved, dropouts diminished, and minorities on and off the campus came to see it as a constructive policy.

I was to work with Bill Gerberding for ten years as vice president for minority affairs. The students kept working on issues such as investment of university foundation funds in South Africa and the effort to merge all ethnic studies programs into a single multiethnic department. Both issues were resolved, only after sit-ins, face-to-face meetings, and the patience of a tolerant board of regents.

Four things happened in all of this that I found instructive. The first occurred during the search for a new vice president for student affairs. I was on the search committee. In keeping the president updated on the pool of candidates, I went to talk to him. The pool was not strong on experience and included my predecessor once removed as vice president for minority affairs. He was known as combative and a person of strong opinions. He would occasionally stop by my office and opine on topics of political concern. The president was not a fan of his. Anyway, the president and I were talking about the letter to go to the campus indicating we were not going forward at this time to fill the search. The debate was over whether we would say postpone the search or suspend it. The president wanted to *postpone*, meaning to put off or delay the search. This left open the hope that the search would be reopened. *Suspend* meant to make inoperable for a time and to stop temporarily but was unclear as to when the search would reopen. After some debate, we agreed that the search would be postponed, since it implied that the search would be reopened. The president got a search with no uprisings, and I got a lesson on grammar. Actually, the president's stance was politically better in that it kept hopes up on the campus and in the external minority communities that persons with vice presidential standing would be competitive in the search.

This was my first learning, and it was that words matter, and care needs to be taken when speaking in behalf of the institution.

The second bit of advice came from a sitting president at a seminar for new presidents offered by the American Association of State Colleges and Universities (AASCU). He began the seminar with the following salvo, "Today is the first day of your firing! If you cannot accept that, you may leave." The temporariness and fragility of acting constructively and according to your personal values was daunting. It made clear that in the midst of all this, you had to gain the skill to know when it is time to go.

The third lesson was taught to me by Bill Gerberding. On the day I got the call from Northern Colorado offering the presidency to me, I remember him calling me into his glass-encased office. He congratulated me and then shut the glass door. He then said, "From this moment on in your presidency, you will act in a glass office. Realizing that all things will be transparent, you alone will make and own the final decision. Keep that in mind."

The fourth piece of wisdom came from Jack MacAllister, a UNC Trustee, whom we will discuss shortly.

Meanwhile in 1991, I was named president of University of Northern Colorado (UNC). Bob Tointon was the chair of the University of Northern Colorado Board of Trustees. He was an investment executive at Phelps Tointon with specialties in transportation networks and highways. When I traveled abroad for the university, I occasionally brought him along, especially to Taiwan, where he had an interest in building new highways of pre-stressed concrete. Tointon's partner was Joseph Phelps of Phelps Winery in Napa, California. These were highly connected business executives with first cabin influence. When Tointon called, the governor answered.

President Herman D. Lujan delivering his inaugural address at the University of Northern Colorado in Greely, 1944.

It was clear that I was not his first choice during the search. Tointon was wary and kept some distance in the beginning. But as we worked together, a thaw began. I had set up a breakfast meeting every Monday with him. The purpose was to keep him informed and to get a sense of the trigger issues on his mind. He also had concerns about the deans. Why were they always on the road and who was managing the college. One dean, the dean of education, was the high visibility dean. He built a national constituency and was out of state very often. The matter caught the governor's eye and some legislators on the education committees. Through the breakfast meetings, I let him know that I thought the dean was not a good fit in the university that was the primary provider of administrators and teachers for Colorado. If I was to move early in my presidency, I needed first cabin support and an honest case. Tointon assured me of the trustee support. I let the governor know of my concern and also the chair of the senate education committee. I spoke with the faculty senate president. I met with the dean and over some months indicated I would make a change. I did and appointed the associate dean as interim. A search followed and ended with appointment of the associate dean to the deanship.

Tointon became a supporter and gave thoughtful advice during his term. He also was generous, giving several million dollars to the Tointon Institute at UNC. The institute was for principals and focused on improving teaching and administrative innovation in top performing schools.

When Tointon stepped aside, Jack MacAllister, chairman (retired) of US West was elected as Tointon's successor. He was a skilled administrator and manager. He was warmly regarded at the company and was a real friend of the university. He personally supported a major scholarship program for needy students. He continued the

Monday breakfasts. His mantra was my fourth learning: "There are no failures, only learnings." On every key issue that came before the university where we did not prevail, he would ask, "What did you learn from this?" I used this practice with other administrators, and we all grew from MacAllister's wisdom. He also was quietly competent and knew how to extract broad ownership of and support for tense issues so that blame would have its limits, if things went wrong. He was a consensus builder.

Not all influencers are friends and supporters. Some can be your enemies and adversaries. The governor of Colorado became an adversary over an appointment to the board of trustees. A trustee published an article in a local Greeley magazine about "no natural fit." The article was about recruiting African American students to UNC at Greeley as there was no natural fit. There were no barbershops, grocery stores, and other personal services in Greeley for African Americans. The article suggested instead that more Hispanics be recruited because there was a local barrio in Greeley that provided a natural fit. The anger over this went off the charts among all minority groups.

I got a call from the governor at 6:00 one morning about this. The trustee was serving a one-year term on the board and wanted to make it permanent. The governor wanted him out because of the outcry he caused. I reminded the governor to take care as appointments required approval in the senate, and there might be limits to his discretionary authority. I urged that he let me look into the whole issue. He did. It was also an election year, and if this had the wrong spin, it would be destructive to the governor's reelection. After talking at length with leaders from all the affected ethnic groups, I found a fit.

I would host a breakfast at the university. Minority leaders and influencers would come. The governor would visit and restate his commitment to minority concerns, and then he would leave. He did as advised and left me to work out a solution. I noted that the interim trustee was filling a temporary one-year term. He could complete the vacancy and the one-year term and not be reappointed. The minority leaders agreed. I called the governor and through his appointment secretary got the Governor's agreement. We announced our intended action, and because the governor had agreed, I indicated that I trusted the governor and gave the leaders my word that the governor would do what he said.

Then came the learning. The trustee did not want to step down. And he also was the chair of the local county Democratic party and used his connections to spread the opposition. Being an election year, the governor, a Democrat, did not want to lose his party's vote. So he blinked. He waited until after the election and then appointed the trustee to a regular term. The minorities felt betrayed. I took much heat. I finally called the governor's office asking that they convey to the governor the breaking of the trust issue. In minority communities, trust is the moral imperative. And he had undercut the trust I had with the minority communities across Colorado. Not happy about my objection, he decided the time had come for a change.

For a number of reasons, five of the seven seats on the board of trustees were also up for appointment. I had asked for a board that could help me raise money as I was set to begin planning for a multimillion-dollar campaign. Instead, I got three attorneys who served in the past as his staff in the governor's office and the wife of the president of the senate (the new appointees needing confirmation in the senate). My resume was already out, and hers was in. She was appointed university attorney. After several years, she was named president, replacing retired US senator Hank Brown who replaced the short-term president Howard Skinner, the dean of music, who replaced me. I ended up as president emeritus and university distinguished professor of business and public policy

Of lesser station but no less valuable were Sherri Moser and Ann Rose. Sherri was my executive assistant at UNC and oversaw the clerical staff. Ann Rose was the head of catering at UNC, helping maintain good relations between the university and the external community. She worked closely and regularly with Carla in the UNC in an effort to build friends between the two communities. An invitation to dine at the president's house was valued. Sherri stood firm in the midst of the havoc surrounding my stepping aside. She gave me intelligence on a daily basis as the tensions mounted. Since she kept the president's calendar, she controlled and used access as appropriate. She had my absolute confidence.

Mary Gates is known worldwide as the mom of Bill Gates III. But in truth, she was the quintessential community leader. She was on the UW Board of Trustees for eighteen years. She was the nudging hand behind the Seattle United Way, and what most do not know, a patroness of minority programs. She was the first trustee to ask to meet me for lunch when I arrived at the UW as its new vice president for minority affairs. She took my measure and urged that I lift the academic performance of minority students at UW. I took the advice and began working on ways to do that. She was always supportive of minority affairs, even when demonstrations flared up over issues such as South African investment of UW foundation funds and the merger of ethnic studies programs on the campus. We lunched from time to time to keep her current on minority issues.

She was very interested in economic development issues in the Seattle area. Early in my tenure, she asked me as chair of the United Way if I would serve as chair of the United Way Committee on Economic Development. The committee worked with Seattle's ethnic and poverty programs and agencies. The committee recommended funding and activities designed to build businesses and sustain support for social programs. It was a job that I found very satisfying and challenging. It gave me access to the top leadership in these areas and gave me a platform to show the university as a true partner in community growth and survival. Mary Gates also was the mother of public civility. When I was appointed president at Northern Colorado, she sent me a pen set and the admonition to keep the good work going in Colorado that we did at the UW. Sadly, I never had the privilege to see her again.

Ada Kirby succeeded Bob Tointon and Jack MacAllister as trustee chair at UNC. She was a vice president at US West and a Cuban refugee who settled in Denver after escaping from Cuba. She was a model for many of the minority students at UNC. She was a supporter throughout my career. She was the only member of the board who really understood what it meant in minority communities to break trust. Our word was no longer our bond. She used her connections with the Latino community to begin rebuilding that trust. I went on the road into minority communities for the university. I brought the top university officials to join me in these efforts.

Ada was helpful. UNC changed its philosophy about recruiting minorities. We went directly to the people and did not rely only on traditional recruitment programs. Our numbers began to grow, and UNC was reaching out to the nontraditional communities. Most importantly, I renovated and found office spaces for the ethnic divisions in OMA. In addition to African American and Hispanic programs, I established Native American Indian and Asian and Pacific Islander programs. My last act as president was to invite Native American leaders from across the state to be my guests at the

President's Home. Nearly a hundred people came, filling the home. I was honored by them as they blessed the President's Home.

I mentioned above that I helped found a program that included Pacific Islanders. Students from Hawai'i had attended in small numbers since the 1950s. I sent a recruiter to Hawai'i to rekindle interest in UNC. I went along. I spoke in high schools across the state telling my story about how a student from Peleau Village could become a university president. The result was the presence of several hundred students from Hawai'i at UNC. This was one of the most gratifying moments in my life. It was second only to my parents watching me get my PhD degree. The third was my inaugural address, which my parents missed as they had passed.

Students can be influential. One such student was Mariano Fiallos Oyanguren. He was a Nicaraguan who had come to the University of Kansas for graduate study. He was from a very well-known Nicaraguan family. His father was Dr. Fiallos Gil, the well-known rector of the Autonomous University of Nicaragua in Leon. Dr. Fiallos Gil had befriended the dictator of Nicaragua, President Somosa, and was able to use that to keep the university autonomous and self-governing

Fiallos Oyanguren studied at the Sorbonne in France and at Southern Methodist University in Dallas. In the classroom, he was brilliant. He had a worldview that American students lacked. He was widely read in Spanish and French, so he brought much to the seminar table of graduate study. I had the great pleasure of being his major professor in his PhD studies. His dissertation work was pioneering, applying the studies of system analysis in biology to the body politic. He used the evolution of the government in Nicaragua as the basis for his work. This was the first application of this theory in the international setting.

He returned to Nicaragua after he completed his degree. He was dean of faculty at Leon. He then served as rector, if my memory serves me right, and moved into government with the Sandinistas. He became chief of the Consejo Electoral, the election council that oversees all elections. He was influential, bringing respect to the office. It is said that when Jimmy Carter brought an outside perspective to the Sandinista election, he found no important irregularities. When the Sandinistas and Daniel Ortega left office, his successor, President Chamorro, kept Mariano on her Consejo Electoral. From Mariano, I learned to consult and listen before acting and hold to my integrity. I played this out in my own presidency and learned that while integrity brings respect, it does not always bring success.

Students can also be teachers. I was fortunate to have really good people study with me. I have already shared the role Victor Ferreros played in my life. I also introduced the Garcia cousins, Ernie, Steve, and Sal Gomez. Steve was the quiet one. He had a good analytic mind. And he was a man of integrity. I met him through his cousin Ernie. He had real promise. So I brought him into the University of Kansas Institute of Social and Environmental Studies, which I directed. In this role, he developed a sense of research and the analysis it requires. This gave him access to research and funded projects. He went on to get his masters and was hired by Vic Ferreros into State Planning and Research, the planning office I had set up. Sal soon joined Steve and Vic, and the Garcia cousins were on their way again.

In no time, Steve left Kansas for Arizona to work for Governor Bruce Babbit of Arizona as an education specialist. I left Kansas in 1978 for the University of Washington as a vice president. I soon realized I needed a budget officer. So I recruited Steve from Arizona to be my budget officer. He fit right into the job and gave me the added advantage of having someone who understood campus student politics. He soon organized the various ethnic programs supporting minority students and helped attract new student leaders and fix programs whose budgets were overspent. While doing this, he applied for and was admitted to doctoral studies in education. This academic side of Steve paid off in the respect he got from the faculty, especially the minority faculty.

The culture in the Office of Minority Affairs had changed from being contentious and problematic to being constructively critical of the office and valuing the academic milieu of a university. The resulting reduction in complaints and demonstrations was largely due to Steve's know-how.

In 1991, I became president of the University of Northern Colorado. It was not very long before I knew I needed a new budget officer. At that time, Steve was completing his dissertation and serving as education policy officer for Washington governor Booth Gardner. I met Booth Gardner at a United Way Jobs Program meeting through Mary Gates. I suggested to Steve that he apply as it was a step up. He did. He was appointed to Governor Gardner's staff as education policy analyst.

The chance to work together in Colorado was attractive. If he came, he could continue his PhD studies, something I had turned into a mantra with him. He came, and with him came his fiancée, Fidelis. And with her came her autistic son whom Steve adopted. I always admired the quiet courage it took to take on such a lifetime responsibility. Steve has always balanced his career with his family life.

Libert O'Sullivan, the kanaka godfather of students from Hawai'i at Saint Mary's, was a much-needed coach for me during my underclass days at the college. An upperclassman, he kept the new freshmen in tow and helped us all stay on track as students. He and I bought an old 1940 De Soto, and it became the kanaka car. Saint Mary's was located in the midst of fruit orchards and cattle grazing land. The sounds of cattle had particular meaning for me. The sounds of the cattle were my lullaby for restful sleep at home in Hawai'i. I could lay my worries on the nightstand and fall into deep sleep. Between Libert and the cattle, I found something familiar to come home to every day. He touched my life personally and became the godfather of my son, Tim.

It is easy to overlook plain folks from the communities which define our immediate world. Two Japanese families impressed me by how they survived World War II and rebuilt their stature in their communities. Paul Hoshiko grew up in Greeley, Colorado, during the Second World War. He and his family were farmers in the Platte River basin. The Hoshikos were known for carrots and onions and built a substantial farm. Hoshiko supported community activities, and I met him on the board of the affiliated banks of Colorado. I served on the committee dealing with the farm and dairy economies of the region. I knew cattle from my days at home on Dad's ranch. I was familiar with dairy farming as I lived near and got milk from a dairy farmer one mile from our ranch. Paul was a strong supporter of the financial needs of the dairies in the area. I learned the ins and outs of dairy and ranch operations and the role a responsible bank plays in their economic success.

Speaking of the Japanese influence in farming, Isamu (Sam) and Kazuko (Kay) Nakao were Nisei born on Bainbridge Island, Washington. They grew up in the Nikkomaki Japanese village on the island. Sam's father was Issei and known as "Slab" Harry. He tended the lumber in the slab pond of the island lumber mill. "Slab" Harry's son met Kay Sakai in Bainbridge. She was the daughter of a

Japanese farmer. They were friends, and the friendship grew. They married in internment camp. They raised three children. Both Sam and Kay helped work the family's strawberry farm. In those days, strawberries were the dominant crop on the island.

When the war came, they were given just a few days to pack and dispose of their property. Sam was able to find a Filipino farmer he knew to take over the farm. Sam and Kay went from Puyallup, Washington, to the Manzanar Camp in Southern California. After their marriage, they wanted to get out of Manzanar. They were able to get transferred to Camp Minidoka in central Idaho to work on a potato farm. When the war ended, they returned to Bainbridge. The farm had been reasonably well kept. So they could start the next chapter in their lives.

Both returned to work for Don Nakata in his grocery store. I met Kay at the grocery counter in Nakata's. I bought daikon pickles, tofu, and pickled plums (*ume*). She inquired as to where I got the taste for Japanese food. I told her Hawai'i. She was very laudable about Hawai'i to me. The next thing you know, she invited me to New Year's Day lunch. Delicacies like *sashimi, tofu*, fishcake, *inari sushi*, and *maki sushi*, every pickle known on earth, and *kanten*, a jello-like dessert. There with *hashi* (chopsticks) poised over Japanese delicacies, I found a friend in Sam Nakao.

We became fishing buddies. He taught me how to fish the fish of the northwest waters. Our chats migrated from fishing tales to discussions about Manzanar and Minidoka and his view of patriotism and civic culture. He spoke often of the Alaska natives and the Clallam and other Washington state Indians who picked his strawberry fields. We chopped wood each fall for the winter. We philosophized about land, water rights, the decline of farming, and racial discrimination. Into his tapestry of life, he wove the view of patriotism as a way to thank a civilization for the public benefits it showered on its citizenry. The idea was that you gave back to the country that nurtured you and your life and the lives of others. These became the images on the tapestry of his life.

There was a lighter side to Sam Nakao. Early one foggy morning, I met him at the pier for our Sunday fishing. It was perfect. The changing of the tide, the risky fog, and signs of fish jumping near the bay combine together to make the fish run. So we headed out of Eagle Harbor to the Puget Sound. We were fishing for silver salmon, so we were going to troll. Sam started cutting the herring bait and told me to get the poles. I reached around the bait box and behold, there were no poles! Sam just shook his head. I looked at him apologetically; I had left the poles at the pier! I chuckled to Sam and said, *"Atama nai,"* which translated from Japanese means something like "empty head." Sam kept shaking his head as he headed to the helm. As he sped toward Eagle Harbor, he finally broke out in an uproar of laughter all the way back to the pier.

As vice president of minority affairs, I met persons from all minority ethnic groups. Two from their ranks were particularly noteworthy. Dr. Norihiko (Nori) Mihara and Michael Castillano. Nori had a PhD in physics from UW and was coordinating the OMA study skills program. He was a son of a *kibei*. Japanese *kibei* are those who were born in the United States but were educated in Japan. Nori's father fit the mold. Upon his return to Seattle, he spent most of his life as the bellboy at the Smith Tower, Seattle's tallest building for many years. As *kibei* do, he raised his son in a strict regimen. Respect and deference were Nori's attributes, and they helped him get his doctorate.

Early in my career as vice president, I felt there was a need for an assistant vice president who focused on academic affairs internally and could tout the OMA to external groups and individuals. Nori had those connections. Moreover, he was seen as a no-nonsense leader in the study skills program. I appointed him assistant vice president for academic affairs.

OMA's external support structure was the Friends of EOP. They raised funds annually through an annual dinner and one or two annual corporate gifts. When I started with Nori to make changes, I strengthened the corporate ties giving us a vehicle for corporate fundraising. Tom Burns and Sheila Voortman were among the friends with contacts in Seattle's business leadership. Andy Reynolds, a television news anchor, gave OMA a public relations dimension it lacked. We also modified the award-giving activities to reflect student interest and stories of their accomplishments. There were few dry eyes after the OMA told their tales of success. When I left OMA for Colorado, the dinner had gone from two hundred or so to over eight hundred in size. Giving had more than tripled under Nori's leadership. This talent for fundraising would linger in my memory until I went to Colorado and began raising gifts from $10 million to $35 million. To get this done, I hired Nori as vice president for university relations.

The second local boy came from Seattle's Filipino community. Michael Castillano was the son of one of Seattle's most respected Filipino business and community leaders. He had a large family, and all of them were upwardly mobile. Mike, as he was called, was well grounded in his home community and used its size and growth as pillars for fundraising and supporting the EOP program. When the burning in effigy hit OMA, it was Mike who kept the Filipino community from actively seeking my removal. Between Mike and Nori, I was able to turn the opposition on campus around and to keep the friends from defecting. This was no small accomplishment.

Two Native American policy wonks were among those supportive of OMA and its Friends of the EOP. They were Bill Demmert and Michael Jennings. Demmert was Tlingit, and he came from one of the two most influential families in Southeast Alaska. He served as director of the Bureau of Indian Affairs under President Nixon. Upon completion of his term, Demmert returned to Alaska and entered higher education at the University of Washington. He was teaching courses in public policy in the School of Public Affairs. I relied on him for advice on Native American education in the field of public policy.

The Office of Minority Affairs (OMA) was a place where Native American students could get advice and counsel. The staff was skilled in helping both urban and reservation students. UW was a large university of thirty-eight thousand, and students from the villages were especially overwhelmed by the size of it all. Villages of two hundred people were considered large. The numbers spoke for themselves. Moreover, university food was not the fare for a tasty Tlingit meal. So on weekends and holidays, students would stay with the counselors or other members of the Native American community for some "real" food and a cultural tune-up. All the while, Demmert was providing academic advice and giving them an insider's view of policymaking.

Demmert was so successful that the governor of Alaska soon approached him to become director of the Fish and Game Commission. Himself a commercial fisherman, the call was too inviting to be turned down. This meant moving to Juneau. And that meant getting his twenty-foot fishing boat to Juneau. By now Demmert and I had become good friends. As a consequence, he asked me to help him take his boat from Seattle to Craig, and thence to Juneau, Alaska, where it was to be docked. I agreed and flew to

Craig, Alaska, to meet him. We visited with his parents and the next day set our twenty footer north to Rocky Pass.

It was a windy morning, and the fish were running so thick that we had to slow our speed to a crawl and maneuver around them. It was a sight to see! Having made it out of the harbor to the open sea, we immediately encountered three- to five-foot swells which was rough going for the twenty-foot hand hewn wooden vessel. We rocked and rolled our way to the inside passage for more protected waters. The strategy worked, and things calmed down.

Our real challenge was to get to Rocky Pass before low tide. Rocky Pass deserved its name. It was sprinkled with rocks all throughout the channel. Low tide would have our bottom scraping along the rocks, and this would be complicated by the kelp beds which would tie the propeller of the twenty footer into engine stopping knots. The result would be a hot boiling engine fighting the kelp thickened bottom and the cadence of rocks ramming along the craggy bottom.

Our solution was to split the dilemma. Demmert knew the boat and had sailed the pass many times. He took the wheel. I could read maps, so I navigated as he piloted. We determined that if we went full throttle, we could just clear the pass before low tide. No more said, we sped off toward a high noon crossing of the pass.

The little boat could have just kept going. As we hit the pass, we cut the throttle by half, and I kept her away from the rocks. But the propeller began pushing against the kelp, and the engine was heating up. We were both worried. I had to keep the kelp away from the prop. I used the oar to push the kelp out of the wake, and the little engine did the rest. We cleared the pass with time to spare.

The next chore was to get to the only fuel station in Frederick Sound. We set our maps and props accordingly and let the boat cut her way to the distant shore. Frederick Sound is a feeding area for whales, both orca and humpbacks. No sooner had we entered the sound when we saw pods of orcas eating and preening. Demmert slowed the engine because the whales were annoyed by the sounds of the engines. The orcas swam along at a distance enjoying their repast, celebrating their fill of krill and romping on the glass smooth water. Seabirds gathered to feast on the fish stirred up by the pods of humpbacks. In no time, we arrived on the western shore, refueled, and moved toward Admiralty Island. Our intent was to anchor in a sheltered bay, fish for our dinner, and sleep watching the expansive starlit sky.

As we found a berthing spot, we anchored and started fishing. It was nearing six o'clock, and the daylight was giving way to evening's entrance and its subtle rays. The trance of the evening was suddenly shaken as a silver fish broke water and leaped toward the sky. It was on Demmert's line and the "pro" tired the prey as he played the line in a dance of twilight's demise. With the day's sunset, the majestic cutthroat cast its last shadow as Demmert brought it in. The fish weighed seven pounds, and combined with roasted corn and fresh bread, it was a first-class feast. We embellished dinner with conversation and visited well into the night.

Demmert and I stayed in touch once he became chancellor of the University of Alaska, Juneau. He eventually ended up at Western Washington University working again for the plight of Alaska's native sons and daughters. The second policy wonk I worked with was a Sioux graduate student who was considering studying at the University of Washington. His name was Michael Jennings. He had been working in the policy area, especially in higher education. He served as a legislative analyst for the University of Alaska system. He was respected in the legislature, enamored of students, and had a keen mind that lurked in the shadow of any discussion. He did not suffer current dogma well. Nor did he condone rhetoric and hyperbole. His belief was that ideas are to be challenged, and then truth will prevail.

Jennings was busy as a director of native studies at the University of Alaska, Fairbanks for quite a few years, bringing stability in that quarter of the campus. He was known as a fair but tough guy, and students had to get their issue honed before taking it to the director. Inside the faculty, he was widely known and generally respected by his colleagues. Over the years, Jennings had become an expert on legislative issues and faculty rights and responsibilities. It was not long before he was working on faculty union rights. He had worked in the chancellor's office and with sister universities on this matter. After several years as faculty representative in several entities, he was hired away by the University of Central Washington as its faculty representative. He was effective but not without opposition among some administrators. He was wooed again, this time by the University of New Mexico where he served as faculty representative until recently.

I worked with Jennings on his efforts to get his PhD. We were able to help him get accepted to doctoral studies at the University of British Columbia in Vancouver. I was privileged to serve as the outside (non-UBC) representative on his thesis committee. He received his doctorate just in time to help him be successful as the changes of his career venues evolved.

Jennings and I became good friends as I followed his career. While he was in Alaska, he invited my son, Tim, and I to join him and his colleague Carl Shepro, a political scientist from the UW, teaching at the University of Alaska at Anchorage. We flew from Fairbanks into the land of the hump tulips and the chillingly clear rivers and lakes of the tundra. We reached a cabin about two hundred miles inland from Fairbanks. We set up our gear and feasted on a light meal. We were out for five days, so we went to bed early, resting for the grueling hunt. For the first day, an American breakfast of bacon and eggs with coffee, stout and hearty, was served, and we were ready for the trek.

The hunt was sluggishly slow. The hump tulips rose and fell unevenly, wearing us to a nub as the day marched on. We were out for bear and moose, the caribou being out of season. We had split into two teams as this is tough and dangerous country anyway, and lone hunters were easy prey for the animals and nature. Jennings and Tim were one pair, and Shepro and I were the second pair. We set locations along the way to touch base and stay coherent no matter what nature and people intended. The sun broke through, sending a blanket of warmth across the tundra. It was a beautiful day, but there was no game.

Suddenly at the river below the ledge we were using as a shield, there appeared a moose cow. She was feeding in the river and ignored us as if we were gnats on the back of an old mother moose. We snapped to and began to move along the hump tulips for a good shot. But as we neared, two things happened. The moose was startled by noises from a distance, indication that another party was after that moose. Second, the moose simply stopped, sniffed, and ran off away from feeding, probably to locate a calf she had tucked away before her feast at the river. This was all of the action for the day. That night we dined porcelain wood stove tucked inside the cabin. The dinner set the stage for recounting the day and making plans for tomorrow's stalk.

For the rest of the week, we saw no tracks worth following; except for our after dinner chats, there was little to tout to anyone. We hunted again in a following year and had no better results. We flew from Talkeetna to a lake several hundred miles away. This time, we camped lakeside and tracked several animals into the hinterlands. We resigned ourselves to being skunked in the hunt but reveled in the intellectual jousts we choreographed each night, gliding from story to story in search of truth.

Jennings and I stay in touch. When I went to the University of Northern Colorado as president, the first thing that caught my eye was the dearth of Native American students and the thin line of courses on the topic. I brought Jennings in as a consultant to analyze and recommend how we could address this shortfall, especially in Colorado's lead university for teaching preparation. Jennings recommended we develop a counseling program and build linkages to the tribes and urban enclaves to increase visibility. We put a counseling program in place based on the UW model and began more intensive recruitment. When I left, I left these programs in place and asked that the president's house be blessed. It was.

At a meeting in Seattle dealing with job opportunities, I met a respected Indian chief. He was Ted George, a Clallam Indian chief who lived in Poulsbo just north of Bainbridge Island. He worked for the federal government in the economic development field. We talked about the need for better access to education and finding the fit between programs and Native American student interests. I worked at getting access to college and required support and Ted dealt with federal programs.

I learned quickly that there are many similarities between Native American culture and kanaka culture: respect for elders, integrity, trust, and sharing. Ted exemplified those and demonstrated by his lifestyle that you can be a professional and still serve your community. Ted became my wise man. We spoke often of the urgency to train the next generation of leaders. We focused on the need to recognize the reality of the reservation and non-reservation Indians. We mulled over the special problems of the reservation youth. We reached no solutions, but each continued to work in his area of specialty. This became a relationship of two professional equals and one cultural un-equal. The chief had the wisdom of long years of native cultural experience which compensated for my inexperience. It gave me pause and helped me be more culturally aware and skilled, particularly when similarities between kanakas and the Native American ways of life were considered.

I also had the great fortune of knowing Viola Hilbert, a Native American elder and one of Washington State's "Living Treasures." She was a teacher of American Indian languages. She was the elder who translated the dying Lushootseed language. She needed support for this effort, and I used my role inside the university to help keep the project going.

She became a leading voice of support for the University of Washington, especially the OMA program. She introduced me to Bernie White Bear, a leader among the Seattle urban tribes. He was politically a respected spokesperson, and his support for me was important and valued. With persons like White Bear, George, and Hilbert, the relationship between my office and the community was interconnected; it brought calm to the differences between the urban and reservation groups. I left OMA with the privilege of being called *siap*. In Lushootseed, it means "friend."

When I left Seattle for Colorado as president of the University of Northern Colorado, Ted and his wife came to my inauguration. He had the noble bearing of a chief at the inaugural lunch. When it came time for some remarks, he struck a noble pose and spoke with the authority of a chief. He thanked me for my service, and in typical Northwest Indian tradition, he chided me about being landlocked in

Colorado which would hamper me in case I had to get out of town in a hurry—be that by choice or by necessity. He then produced a miniature hand-carved canoe, a beaded neck bracelet, a paddle, and a cedar leaf with advice to head for the nearest river, wear the necklace for protection, use the paddle for speed, and the cedar to guide me home to the northwest. Always the jokester, Chief Ted had struck again.

And then there is Mustafa Dhada. Sculptor, author, political scientist, educated by Jesuits, honed by St. Catherine's, and fluent in seven languages. He was born in Mozambique and is the father in a household of five. He is a first cabin scholar with the ability to see beyond the early layers of conflict to the core conflicts and controversies that characterize the real nub of the issue. He has been a valued colleague whose world-based perspective helps keep those with whom he has contact anchored in the inner core. He does not suffer fools or dogmatists well.

I appointed him the lead strategic planning for the University of Northern Colorado because of his broad perspective. Many UNC faculty had been at UNC for most of their careers. Anchored in the shadow of the Rocky Mountains, they were insulated socially and academically. A small research university with ambitions, UNC needed scholars with their best years still ahead of them. Dhada was one of them. This left him with few friends in his department and isolated; thus he left UNC for Clark University, Atlanta, where my former KU student Walter Broadnax was president. Dhada was a scholar there for several years and eventually moved to Los Angeles Alliant University in Southern California. He has since served as Dean of Extended Learning at California State University, Los Angeles, and associate vice president at California State University, Bakersfield.

The influencers were wide and varied. Someone who could span the range of expectations and provide straight and thoughtful advice was essential for these attributes to be meaningful. James Collier was just the person to fill that bill. We met at Kansas University where he was directing university relations, and I was directing the Institute for Social and Environmental Studies (ISES). His first impression was underwhelming. He was about standardization of logos and letterheads. ISES used the sunflower as background and light brown tinted imagery of the sunflower, the Kansas state flower. Over several discussions, I came to recognize the importance of logos and how to coordinate materials for the public eye in ways to garner support for the institution. I had the ISES logo and wheat-colored paper replaced by a logo Collier found acceptable.

Our paths crossed after I left KU for the University of Washington, and Collier had gone from Kansas to the University of Illinois. There he worked for Bill Gerberding as the lead person in university relations. The newly hired Gerberding wanted his own university relations team led by Collier. This became especially important to Gerberding as the university was about to embark on a multimillion-dollar fundraising campaign. Collier was hired after a search, and Collier was appointed vice president for university relations. OMA became a headache for Collier as the students were active and multi-issued. They kept raising issues before the board of regents over such things as the investment of foundation funds in South Africa and opposition to the merging of ethnic studies units into a single department.

Throughout these turbulent times, Collier and I kept conversations going on behind the scenes, trying to balance regent concerns and student interests. We abided by a policy of no surprises. In crises, Collier helped keep conversations open and respectful, a key to conflict resolution. I left for Colorado, and Collier would leave the UW soon enough.

I was busy rebuilding the UNC political milieu. Faculty conflict with campus leadership and the board of trustees left a wake in need of coordination. Collier came to mind immediately. The only problem was that Collier was still at the UW. But sooner rather than later, it became clear that Gerberding's successor was moving for a change in Collier's portfolio. I had a search underway for this position as Nori Mihara was leaving to spend a year at the American Council on Education (ACE). He was to focus on Asian Americans in higher education, a project to strength his career path and begin a pathway nationally to address this topic.

I was readying UNC for a major fundraising effort, and Collier had helped Gerberding through that process at UW. On the campus, there was the need for integrating change to PhD status. This also required funding priorities, for there was little by way of internal funds in the instructional budget. There was also the expectation that research support increase to befit PhD level scholarship. These were all activities that Collier had experienced at a major graduate and research university.

I called Collier and urged him to fly in so key campus constituents could interview him. He flew in and interviewed. He told me that just before he left for Colorado, the new president called him into his office and informed Collier that he was removing him from the vice presidency. I was Collier's only immediate hope. We talked about the problems he would likely encounter. The next day, he left, and the campus constituents were all accepting of Collier. I called Collier and offered him the job. He accepted and flew to Bill Gerberding's retirement celebration the next day and announced Colliers appointment to a cheering crowd at the UW faculty Club.

Collier immediately went to work. He talked to trustees, campus leaders, student ideas, the Colorado Press Corps, and other vice presidents he knew, and he got directly into the athletic program. The immediate issue at hand was a growing momentum among some donors for moving football from NCAA Division 2 to NCAA Division 1. Collier's seasoned hand grasped the top issues. I was now free to deal with other existing issues.

The vignettes and stories of this chapter are about the people who have touched my life and how varied their impacts on my life have been. Their backgrounds have ranged from fishing to philosophy and their perspectives from the plain to the panache. I shared influencers to show that people vary in how they affect others. Some influence and have no idea that they are influencing. Most are modest and respectful about how they affect others. With this in mind, I turn now to the core values and ideas derived from them that helped me weave the tapestry of my life.

Chapter Eleven

The Learned and Good Person

Na'auao A Maika'

Your mana is the tapestry of your life, and its centerpiece is the learned and good person. In the kanaka way of life, each of us has a set of values and beliefs that we blend together through our life choices. And these choices are what keep mana evolving and growing as we live out our lives. In western thinking, we tend to divide life into two spheres: the rational and the affective, or the mind of the scientist and the emotions of the psychologist. The kanaka tradition blends these into a single process which adapts and changes as we do. Thus, the learned man is also the good person.

The *na'auao* is the learned one, and *maika'i* is the esteemed and righteous one. The blending is symbolic in how we name these values. The western culture speaks of the intellect and the heart. The kanaka speaks of the *na'au* or intestines where mind and body blend as the center of life. *Na'auao* is to be learned as the scientist and wise as the philosopher. *Maika'i* is to be righteous in the sense of being just and moral. The challenge for me was to become a learned and good person. Such a person is *lokomaika'i* or generous and sharing. Part of this idea is like the western saying, "To whom much is given, much is expected." Sharing also has another meaning. It was one my father held. His idea was that you learn by sharing what you know. You teach by making the circle of knowledge larger when you are generous about what you know. When you share your knowledge, all human knowledge about that subject is enriched. So when we share our individual expertise, the whole society's knowledge about the subject is lifted to excellence.

How does a learned and good person act in life? Kanakas learn from their young days that learning begins with *ho'olohe*, listening. Typically youth listen to the teacher and kupuna as they share their expertise. Respect for the kupuna is at the base of learning. Listening leads to *maopopo* or clarity and understanding. Learning should be plain and clear if understanding is to occur. Understanding and comprehension take time, so kanakas should be *manawanui* or patient. To be *manawanui* is to let time be a partner in learning. Use original sources in classes where possible, give lectures strategically, and let conversation emerge, so students can share what they know. I set up seminar or "talk story" times in class, dividing students in groups for class discussions and in their research, which I required in the syllabus. My time teaching at St. Louis High in Honolulu formed the base for my approach at the university level. I added tutorials at key points in a class, so students and I could converse individually about their situations and problems. When you treat students as partners in learning, they invest in the success of the course. By letting those who have skill work with those that do not, everyone learns more. They all become smart (*akamai*).

Among the things needed in an approach to learning and teaching is the resolution of conflict. Intimate societies like the 'ohana have conflicts. Some are very profound and threatening to the 'ohana. Over the years, kanakas have developed a process for finding peace and making things right.

Ho'oponopono is a process to make things right. As pointed out earlier, the process depends on an independent third party or leader. The leader clarifies the conflict by having each side set forth their grievance directly to the leader. The points of high conflict are identified. Each party makes its case without blaming and direct confrontation. The points which the conversation finds as possible negotiable are uncovered. By moderating the conversation, the leader moves the conversation toward resolution, identifying and focusing on elements that can be used to build a resolution. Step by step, the third party walks the grievers through this and helps piece together a solution. Through conversation (rather than confrontation), an acceptable solution is identified. Both grievers have a stake in the resolution and mutual forgiveness occurs to end the process. While emotions can run high, the neutrality of the leader keeps things even handed by having to communicate through the leader. It is a process that is much more like diplomacy than using direct political power to reach a mandated solution. Many kanakas avoid conflict as much as possible. So power is not seen as the tool of first resort. It produces winners and losers and is not mutual in its impact. Some people can hold a grudge for a long time. Approaches that consider this are more likely to endure. I have learned additionally that the kind of conversation that ho'oponopono channels also has its uses in teaching and learning.

Pono is a powerful moral imperative. It teaches that morality legitimizes and makes things right. That is the driving notion behind leadership. The good leader builds agreements mutually, and there is joint ownership of the solution and of the obligation to make things right.

Of all the concepts described here, there are three concepts that have guided me through life. They are *malama, mahalo,* and *makamaka. Malama* is the first of these. It means to civilize and enlighten those around you, especially your students and those whom you consider to be your mentees. One who leads by making the circle of knowledge larger is *malama*. One who protects others and is loyal is *malama*.

The second guiding concept is mahalo. It is commonly used in thanking someone. Next to *aloha*, mahalo it is the most common of words used by tourists. In the context of these reminiscences, it means esteem and respect. A good person is one who conducts his or her life in ways that engender esteem and respect. My father was mahalo. He was widely respected among the independent cane planters and ranchers on the Big Island. His employees held him in high esteem. He was *pa'a*, a person of fidelity. This is behavior I strive for day by day.

The third word is *makamaka*. To be *makamaka* is to be an intimate and trusted friend in whom one can confide freely. We all need people with whom we can talk and are able to do so without worry that confidences would be broken. Chief Ted George was *makamaka*. So were the members of the Saint Mary's and Saint Joseph brotherhoods, especially Frank Urias, Alf Collins, Mike Mase, Dave Neitling, Odell Johnson, and Ron Sceglio, all of Saint Mary's, along with Cliff Rezentes and Frank Ferreira, both of Saint Joseph.

These are the behaviors that help to hold families together through the trust they build and the sense of shared responsibility that they breed. They are essential to maintaining intimate relationships. And they are at the core of real and enduring personal friendship. In the professional world, it applies to employer and employee relations. It is at the core of corporative fairness in business competition. It pertains as well to diplomacy in the political world and the behavior of states and governments. In all of these areas, saying what you mean and doing what you say leads to respect. It is at the heart of being a good and respected person.

I need closure when all of these values are present. I expect that everything is as it should be when I am finished with an activity. To me, things are not complete unless everything fits. Kanakas say it is *pololei*. It is done as we wanted it done, and there are no loose ends.

I have applied these ideas as best I could in over forty-five years as a teacher and administrator. I have had good days and bad days. I had my integrity as a learned and good person tested. I have had my differences with trustees, governors, university presidents, university senates, faculty, and students in my professional life. The most recent conflict was at a campus of the California State University, where I was interim provost. I supported the president in a move by the faculty to vote "no confidence" in the president. Because I would not go along, I was censured by the senate. There is no such element as formal censure in the CSU rules and regulations. They did not want to vote "no confidence" in me, so they came up with the milder notion of censuring me.

There have been some good things over the years that are worth remembering. My alma mater, Saint Mary's College of California, gave me a PhD in the humanities in recognition of my years of service in furthering undergraduate studies and the liberal arts. And more recently, I have had the privilege of serving my alma mater and its president, Brother President Ronald Gallagher, over a two-year period, working to help reposition the college and its mission in these rapidly changing times.

In 1993, Taiwan Municipal Teachers College honored me by planting a cypress tree in my honor at its entrance. The college is one of the largest of Taiwan's teachers colleges. Its president Dr. Mao (deceased) and former president Hwan Kun-Huei honored me for my work in teacher education in Colorado and Taiwan. This living tree carries the obligation to continue this work and good relations. The most gratifying effort to recognize my work as a president was the naming of Lujan Hall, a residential dormitory on the University of Northern Colorado campus. On October 2, 2005, the naming ceremony took place. Some friends and students attended. It was an appreciated gesture and remains a reminder of why many of us turn to education for our life's work.

If there is a need to summarize what I have shared with you, it comes from a saying on the back plate of the chair the University of Washington gives its leaders as they leave the university. In my case it reads:

> "Ally of the disadvantaged
> Dedicated leader and teacher
> Flak Catcher extraordinaire."

Chapter Twelve

Sweet Home

Ku'u Home

It is here in this narrative that I turn to a dear friend of the 'ohana, one who has been able to keep Hawaiians alive for our generation. That friend is Father George De Costa. I use his story here within this chapter because to me, he is the example for those of us in Hawai'i who have been able to cope with change. George became a priest in the midst of turmoil and change in the church and in Hawai'i. He was a leader and change agent in the Hawai'i Catholic Church. He was able to remind all of us about the best in Hawai'i, to hold on tightly to the language, the culture, the literature, and the music. He was able to lead us in embracing change harmoniously, thereby avoiding religious and social chaos and havoc. He has and always will be an inspiration to those of us who have learned to think and ponder before we act, to look for the good in change, and to not lose sight of what is important—the features that define us as Hawaiians. Both George and his deacon Joe Camacho recite the phrase that keeps us grounded: *okamae, uahala, uahala ia*. Or to translate the idea of the phrase as best I can from ancient Hawaiian: Keep the chaos of the past there. Be in the present. Being in the present brings peace.

Sweet home is also where the ʻohana thrives. It is the anchor point for extended families. Lucas Lujan knew that, and he built a home where the ʻohana could flourish. He built a four-bedroom wood frame plantation house. The plantation carpenters helped Lucas build it. By the 1880s, the house was full. It came to be called by some as the "big house." Remember that Kaililau bore thirteen children. Most lived at one time or another in the big house. The house faced west and bordered the Old Government Road. The lot was an acre in size. Its location on the lot was exquisite with flowering bushes and their morning and evening fragrances, especially the sweet night-blooming cereus. At twilight, the night-blooming cereus petals opened, releasing their gentle scent, whispering to the dayflowers that night was on its way.

Lujan family home in Peleau, 1959.

Life began each morning with the dawn of the orange sunrise and the lingering fragrance of white gardenias and jasmine. The morning sun danced in its rays, leaping across the sugarcane leaves, wet from the beaded morning showers. The rays languished as droplets, landing in the shade of the French mango tree at the edge of the back wall of the big house. The wind pushed a ballet of drops up the wall. Then with a plié sprinkled the drops through the open windows and on to the colorful Hawaiian quilts Kaililau had sown. The dampness this brought was nature's way of waking everyone with grace and hope for a brighter day.

A breakfast meal sat on the counter, its places already set. Leftovers were a daily part of the morning meal. Poi, beef stew, and fresh papaya or mango were typical fare. Saloon Pilots (a type of hardtack cracker favored by sailors) topped the meal off. They were great dunking crackers for the coffee or tea that gave finish to the meal. Folks ate heartily and set out for their appointed day well fueled and satiated.

The house had four bedrooms and four to eight people resided in them at any one time. The bedrooms had bedding for eight, each with quilts from the hands of Kaililau. Many homes of this vintage had an outhouse and a cesspool. But disposing of waste was not a flip of the wrist matter. The big house had indoor plumbing and a short pipe to the cesspool for disposal. It was adequate for the standards of the day.

The kitchen was ample, fueled by a kerosene stove and lights. Bread was baked fresh during the week and especially on Friday for the weekend. Poi was also pounded three or so times a week, allowing the poi to sour, as the kanaka favorite was day-old poi with its sour tangy taste. Fruits and vegetables were fresh from the garden plot near the big house. Sweet potato was the mainstay along with Portuguese squash (pipinoles), the squash's leaf tips, papaya, breadfruit, watercress, avocado, and salted fish. Rice was also kept in twenty-five-pound bags. As canned foods developed, they were ushered into the cupboards and eventually onto the everyday menu.

What was set on the table began life in the backyard with its vegetables, especially taro, sweet potatoes, various squashes, corn, and tomatoes. Fruit was always handy. Most common were mango and papaya fresh from the backyard. Also fresh and a staple was the breadfruit. It was eaten in many ways. It could be boiled and mashed into poi or baked like a potato. Or when ripe, it could be cut open and baked to a brown crust then eaten as one would a ripe squash.

Speaking of poi, there were three ways to prepare it. The usual way was to boil and then pound the taro corm with a stone pestle and a stone mortar. This poi would then age, so each could have it as they liked it. A second type of poi was sweet potato poi. It was also boiled and pounded into a mash. The last type of poi came from the breadfruit. It was also boiled when half ripe and pounded into a creamy three-finger poi.

The garden edged against the chicken coop and yard. The manure was used as fertilizer for the garden. A pig or two served as nature's walking disposals. Their pen was located at the southernmost side of the big house property, draining off into the sugarcane field. There also was a small pasture for the horses, and a heavy galvanized pipe served as the anchor for the tethered horses. The horses were often tied to graze along the roadside and shoulder of the Old Government Belt Road. The horses kept the Belt Road clean, and this provided fresh grasses for the horses. It was good for both sides.

A row of coconut trees bordered the North Hilo side of the property from the Old Government Road to the eastern corner of the lot. The row began with the common coconut and ended with three

Samoan coconut trees laden with fruit. The Samoan coconut trees provided larger and sweeter fruit and were a shorter tree, making them easy to climb. These trees were prolific. The coconuts were large in size with half a gallon of juice in a single coconut, ample thin meat in the coconut's developing stage, and thick tender meat in the full grown coconut. The remaining coconut provided a spongy fist-sized seed that stored remaining juice as the coconut matured, and this was called the palm. The 'ohana never ran out of coconuts at any stage of the coconut's growth.

The remaining yard had tamarinds, guavas, a Hawaiian mango tree, a hybrid mango tree, pomulo, star fruit, avocados, a lone tangerine tree, bananas of several varieties, and it ended with a beehive yielding honey every year. Raising thirteen children was no romp in the yard. Lucas Lujan decided to build some simple one- or two-room bungalows to handle the overflow, caused largely by the fact that spouses added husbands and children of their own. From the porch of the big house, you could see the small houses. A one-room house was built on the Hamakua side of the French mango tree. To the right, and therefore the South Hilo side, a large one-room bungalow was constructed. Another larger bungalow was built on the southwest corner of the lot at the juncture of the Old Government Road and 'Awapuhi Stream.

Every agriculture operation requires tools. Lucas knew this, of course, and he built a shop on the South Hilo side of the lot. It had a concrete floor, a recess for a fuel tank, and a gasoline hand pump. Large workbenches ran along the inside walls, and tools were hung or stored under the benches. Lucas and Samuel Ho'olohekamohoali'i made daily use of the shop and the collection of tools accumulated over the years. The shop also functioned as a tack house for the horse saddles and other equine paraphernalia. Beef was hung there to cure and age before butchering.

Lucas Lujan had built a family compound: a self-contained village where family life was at the core. 'Ohana had their social and economic pathways to making a living, while the 'ohana gave them respite when their personal mana was under scrutiny or being challenged. Ho'oponopono was an available tool for conflict resolution. Mahalo (respect) required civility (malamalama) and righteousness (mana). The 'ohana was a living daily experiment that helped you find yourself. It gave each member the time, place, and ability to blend personal values with an environment of broad social and communal values. This ability to strike a balance between personal and social values was essential for a race living in the in between.

Chapter Thirteen

For the Children

Na Keiki

It was one of those pristine sunny days at Peleau. The morning showers had scrubbed the clouds and left their shadows dancing on the waving Pangola grass. The hour was one past noon when shadows stood straight up, and it was the time when Samuel Ho'olohekamohoali'i was readying to take his daily ride up the plantation road and across the *kuleana* pastures as the *nana 'aina* or line rider would do, checking the fence and water troughs along the way. While the horse was having its way in ranching, Samuel Ho'olohekamohoali'i was driving his trusty old 1954 Packard rather than riding my horse, Radio. He was also taking along one of his grandchildren, Keithan, for a ride and an hour or so of "talking story" with *kuku* (grandpa). It was a time for a quiet and tenderly elder to share stories and ideas with the next generation.

Samuel Hoʻolohekamohoaliʻi sat Keithan next to himself on the front bench seat and turned the key. The dashboard came to life, its green lights flashing from door to door. The engine awakened as the automatic transmission slid forward. The ride had begun. Samuel Hoʻolohekamohoaliʻi drove to the plantation road that paralleled the Lujan *kuleana* boundary and then crossed the right of way he had agreed to with the plantation and parked where the *kuleana* road crossed the plantation road. Their intersection was at the crest of the rolling hills and tall grass of the pasture. It was the perfect perch.

The cattle meandered by on their way to the water trough in the paddock. This was part of their ritual of survival, watering up before resting and chewing their cud in the afternoon shade under the sprawling banyan tree. As the cattle walked by, they were close enough to touch. Young Keithan reached out of the open window and patted the backs of the shameless young Herefords, laughing with glee. Anticipating questions, Samuel Hoʻolohekamohoaliʻi would talk about the cattle. He described the *paʻeke* (corral) and how it was used to sort out cattle, how it was used in branding, and its role in the spraying of the cattle as an antidote to deal with flies and other airborne and external illnesses. The lesson for the day always included the *pa uwea* (wire fencing) and why paddocks were used rather than simply letting the herd graze across the whole ranch.

Herman in pasture at Lujan farm and ranch as teenager.

Sometimes Samuel Ho'olohekamohoali'i would talk about raising cane. He described the use of water diversion ditches and would point out the meandering nature of the ditch. By slowing water through its curves, the speed of the water was reduced, and this kept the soil from being washed away. He explained why mechanization of the sugar industry was damaging to the economy and the environment. He did this without preaching or thinking that the grandchildren would want that level of detail in their tender age. So he showed what a ditch was and where the water that drained went.

His lesson on cane planting was kept simple. Use curving rows. Plant variety that generated long stalks as they have more canes per plant. Spray pesticides carefully. Use trucks and machines that damage fields minimally. The final note in his story was the central role of conservation.

The visits always included a story of one kind or another. One he liked to tell was the story of Kamohoali'i, the royal selected one who had the ear of the gods and the one for whom Samuel Ho'olohekamohoali'i was named. So the story goes that Kamohoali'i was the favorite brother of the goddess Pele and accompanied her from Kahiko, the land of old. He had two forms, shark and human. He was an ancestral shark god. There was a game played called Malama-ki that was played only in Malama-ki Puna, Hawai'i. The player would hold a Ti leaf in his hand and chant, "That Ti, this Ti my Ti is for Kamohoali'i, to fly!" If the wind was right and the chant correctly done, the Ti would fly off and return. The game was quite like the paper airplane game we played as youngsters. We folded paper into likenesses of airplanes and then launched them by hand. They would return if the right model had been folded together. The story told Samuel Ho'olohekamohoali'i' headed for Kuu Home.

Samuel Lujan admires Arizona oranges where he represented Hawaii's Soil Conservation program.

Lujan Farm and Ranch officially named by Soil Conservation district. Samuel Lujan is on the right.

Of all the awards and recognition he received, none was as cherished as the charter membership he held in the Mauna Kea Soil Conservation organization. It brought him many opportunities to tell the soil and water conservation story to the general public and to those leading the ranching and sugarcane businesses. He was active in setting up site visits to model projects along the Hamakua Coast. He developed a friendship with Richard Penhollow, the Parker Ranch manager. He worked closely with Dr. Edward Hosaka of the Department of Tropical Agriculture at the University of Hawai'i and its extension programs, providing cane planters and ranchers with assistance as they addressed soil and water issues, animal health and productivity, new varieties of plants, grasses, and breeding. Samuel Ho'olohekamohoali'i carried out many of these ideas and practices, including water diversion ditches, contour planting, pioneering the use of Pangola grass and intense grazing in five-acre paddocks, improving pig feed practices with his Duroc Jersey pigs, and experimenting with varieties of sugarcane that were more productive than variety 1063. Samuel Ho'olohekamohoali'i became known as a "zealous conservationist." The *Hilo Tribune Herald* of May 11, 1969, page 11, described him this way:

> The passing of Samuel Hoolohe Lujan, long acting in promoting and encouraging the advancement of Big Island agriculture, leaves an immense void in the ranks of soil and water conservationists of the 50th State. Sam, as he was known by a wide circle of friends and associates locally and throughout Hawai'i, was an active and dedicated proponent of conservation.
>
> He enlisted early in the cause of conserving the Big Island's agriculture when he became a charter member of

Mauna Kea Soil and Water Conservation District, largest district on the Island and in the State. He was one of the organizers of the district in 1955 and was appointed to the district's board of directors at the time of organization.

For nearly 13 years, until June 1968, he served in that capacity. During that time, he held the office of chairman twice, for a year and a half in 1963–64, and again during the final year of his service, 1967–68. Thus, for nearly a decade and a half, he gave generously and vigorously of his time and effort in promotion of soil and water conservation.

Lujan devoted his entire life to agriculture, having been born, brought up, and lived his entire life on a ranch. He developed his holdings into a 200- to 300-acre ranch which was divided about evenly between raising sugarcane and cattle.

Conservation projects which he carried out on his own which contributed to his ranching success included installation of water reservoirs, rotation grazing, and pasture fertilizing.

Sam's father also has been a Big Island rancher. But that came later to the elder Lujan. He arrived here a Portuguese sailor but jumped ship and remained to become a farmer.

As Hawai'i's delegate to the annual western regional meeting of the National Association of Soil and Water Conservation Districts in December 1962, Sam did a real job of missionary work. He so successfully dispensed *aloha* at the Sacramento meeting that he was able to convince convention delegates to designate Hawai'i for the 1963 convention.

During his 1962 trip to the convention on the mainland, Sam also was an invited guest at the annual program at the Goodyear Tire and Rubber Company's conservation farm near Phoenix, Arizona.

This six-day, all-expense-paid tour remained a highlight in Sam's recollection, and it fortified his zeal in pushing local conservation.

(It should be noted here that Sam's father, Lucas Lujan, was a Spaniard and not a Portuguese).

Samuel Ho'olohekamohoali'i was a man before his time. He was immersed in conservation and concern for the environment. He was green before it became a fad.

His partner in leading change was education. He himself had turned to education at age twelve. He graduated from high school when he was twenty-four and developed an interest in science and in research and experimentation. He stepped aside, so Alice could go to normal school and thence to get her master's degree in New York, in spite of wagging tongues that she would never come back. Well, she did, and her marriage was the better for it.

Alice took her talents into the classroom as soon as she returned from New York. As a field assistant and district director for speech and reading, she carried a philosophy of being where the students are, not where we wish them to be. She saw students not as problem speakers or readers but as partners in solving these two problems. She saw stories and the cultural affinity for telling stories as the bedrock for resolution. The teller of tales was now the weaver of a new syntax, displacing pidgin. She would compare standard terms, then contrast the pidgin involved with the new syntax. In short, talking story in the pidgin that overlay the "proper" word became the stepladder for the new learning of the proper word.

Mother's techniques made sense to me. So when I came home from St. Mary's College to teach at St. Louis High School in Honolulu, I was given those students who were labeled lower ability students (defined by the use of the Stanford-Binet test). They were poor readers and speakers and tended to come from lower social status groups. Their textbooks were not easy to fathom for most of these students. In American history class, I set the selected textbook aside and used it as a source of ideas to inform our discussions and analyses. I placed the first chapter on the founding of the United States with the constitution itself and some of the federalist papers. Each night, students did a reading from original sources and wrote a short paragraph on what the message of the documents was. The next day in class, students were grouped into learning groups and discussed their work and made corrections along the way. Over time, the learning was noticeable, and the discovery of new syntax was the subject of class discourse. Students were reading better and writing more systematically.

Epilogue

If Abe Pi'ianai'a were still alive, he would probably give more focus to the personal virtues that matter in life. As already discussed, first among them is malamalama (civility), pono (fitting and orderly), makamaka (intimate friend), mahalo (respect and esteem), ho'omana (empower), and mana (righteousness). You find yourself by giving attention to the mix of these that fits your mana.

The challenge for the next generation lies in gathering the ideas of elders, reading about kanaka history and culture and keeping some kanaka language alive. Find kupuna and keep the conversations ongoing. Mine their minds. Let the young ones listen as the elders tell their stories.

The Lujan 'ohana has focused on education of the *keiki*, the children. The *makua* generation went to school, and Lucas Lujan and Kaililau especially stressed completion of their studies. Going to school was the family goal. He was in his the eighties and retired, but that made no difference in his commitment to education. On the other side of the alliance, the Ignacios, the majority became teachers and then principals. The last of the Ignacio *makua* teachers passed in 2012.

Then came the *kuakahi*. The *kuakahi* generation focused on going beyond college. Herman and Leilani got PhDs; Carla, like Alice, got a master's. Kaleo obtained a degree in agriculture economics. Leilani's two other boys and Herman's three went as far as high school; her eldest son, Kevin, has a master's degree in psychology, and her youngest, Kristian, has master's degree in language and literacy and is a respected mentor teacher in his district. Kenneth is a respected police office on the Big Island who brings his talent of negotiation to his daily work. He and his wife Leslie value education as Samuel and Alice Lujan did. They work tirelessly to encourage their three sons to pursue their educations with curiosity and joy.

Behind the *kuikahi* generation comes the *kualua*. Tim's two sons TJ Timothy Samuel Lehua was in biology and chemistry, and Cody Kahikolu was in the business school. Both graduated from college. Finally, Leilani has a *kuakolu* granddaughter from Kristian, and Herman has a *kuakolu* granddaughter from Cody Kahikolu named Iwa kaleiho'olohe kamohoali'i a me ho'opomaikai, "the one who brings the families together and does so with grace and beauty." As we know, tied to the land. And in the case of Hawai'i, it is pertinent, and the 'ohana is threatened by outside forces. There have been several major incidents: Ni'ihau and Kaho'olawe, where people have bought an island. In 1864, the Robertson family purchased Ni'ihau from Kamehameha V.

The Robinson's strategy was to keep Ni'ihau pristine, and limiting access was its tactic. Preservation of an aging lifestyle has guided them. The people live as they always have, keeping customs and language authentic and acting as preservers of tradition and discourse. People may come for half day visits. The grandsons of the family currently govern, seeking consensus from the people when issues arise and keeping the island 'ohana active and vibrant.

Kaho'olawe is by comparison another story. The island is currently governed by the Kaho'olawe Island Reserve Commission. It is held in the commission for the next sovereign nation leader should the island be declared a sovereign nation. The two points of view about future use are in deep conflict. The island is most known for its role as a target site for US military bombing practice during World War II.

Now comes another purchase of a whole island. In August, 2012, high tech guru Lawrence J. Ellison, Oracle CEO, bought the property from Castle & Cooke, an economic leftover company from the pineapple king days of Castle & Cooke. Castle & Cooke owned 95 percent of Lana'i. The island grew pineapples for the world market. But the company was not always economically sensitive. When it left Lanai, the island was covered with black vinyl, used by the company to keep weeds down and nutrients in. Environmental waste practices had not yet taken root.

According to the *San Francisco Chronicle* of October 4, 2012, Ellison has an evolving vision of what Lana'i will become. He calls it his little laboratory for experimenting with improving the environment to make it more compatible with evolving notions of green living. He intends to convert seawater into freshwater, see more people using electric cars, and increase fruit exports, especially to Japan. So far, there is no plan of action but goals that suggest some semblance of the respect for and importance of how to treat the 'aina.

The next example of a large purchase and investment in Hawaii's crumbling post–World War II economy was Henry J. Kaiser of Kaiser Industries which included Kaiser Steel and shipbuilding. He invested in the infrastructure of Hawai'i, both physical and social. The Kaiser Hospital at Ala Moana exemplifies the Kaiser social agenda of being a partner in serving social needs as a part of the economic development process. Kaiser showed that partnership rather than exploitation can be a viable economic option.

So what can we look forward to as the transformation takes place? Will culture be kept vibrant and in mind as a key pathway to change? Will the pursuit of profits and economic choices emerge as the center pieces for transformation? Will the land become a Macau, a Singapore, or a floating Las Vegas? Who will lead the path of transformation if profits are modest in that economic sector? Except for entertainment, there are few things in which the kanakas may excel. In what skills will kanakas be retrained to fit better in the economics of technology and science? Ellison is a tech guru. There are economic opportunities which can include the interface of culture and economics. Whatever emerges better not repeat the careless exit of the sugar and pineapple companies and their development of an economy of monopolies rather than partnerships.

For the 'ohana, the underlying issue is land use and an economically viable active farm and ranch. It is modest in size, so the 'ohana must be efficient in its land use. The land has evolved from an *ahapua'a* to sugarcane to a cattle ranch. Like his grandfather, Tim has been innovative. He extended the soil conservation practices of his grandfather, resolved water catchment issues in the 'aina, and brought soil conservation practices into his grazing plan. He adjusted the use of 'Awapuhi Stream to new water use practices.

He studied cattle breeds, and after getting the views of ranchers and animal and soil scientists, he brought in the beef master breed. This breed is found in humid East Texas and thrives in the moist tropical climate of Peleau. He revived the use of Pangola grass on the ranch, resulting in market-ready cattle in less than a year.

Tim's sons, TJ Lehua and Cody Kahikolu, are already living their experience about life at Peleau. Unlike many kanakas, the Lujans have not sold the land. The land is the promise for the future—their future.

Promising futures have prodigious pasts. May 2, 2011, was a day of fame for those who call Hawai'i *nei*—home—no matter where they live geographically. A president born in Hawai'i and relatives of a soldier born on Maui gathered in the White House on that day for a Medal of Honor ceremony. Two "local boys," as we say in Hawai'i, would share the limelight for our race and act in our behalf to make May 2 a "Day of Fame," not infamy.

Anthony T. Kaho'ohanohano of Wailuku was recognized with the Medal of Honor for his valor under fire in the Korean War. He saved his company by giving cover fire for his troops as they were overcome. He used a machine gun. And when it ran out of ammo, he turned to hand-to-hand combat. He ended using a shovel as a weapon to stop them. His men made it to safety; he did not.

One more loss of a dying race. But that is where 'ohanas come into play. They connect generations. They pass on the values that matter. The bonds that bind. And in this case, his inoa (Kanaka name) gave all of this special meaning. *Ho'ohanohano* means "to bring honor and glory." And he did—to his family, to his friends, to all of Hawai'i, and to the nation. An offstage TV camera still audible heard the president of the United States tell George Kaho'ohanohano (Anthony's nephew) to give his *aloha* to a cousin of George's with whom the president went to school. The president said, "Tell him I said, 'How's it'!" That is pure local kanaka talk!

Looking out over the wild marsh of San Francisco Bay by my mainland home, and rummaging through the attic of my mind, on this day, I found life in the midst of death and a perspective about being kanaka. Blood is finite, but culture is not. Is Hawaiian a dying race? It is, if we only look at bloodlines. Is it a dying race? Not if you see it as culture, as a way of living. Kanakas are a paltry few in the growing numbers of the human race. We are a decimal if we are even counted among the billions. But looking at it as culture, we see the kanaka 'ohana growing in number. Our culture is our future.

I see it now, as I reflect over the layered tapestries of our culture and the collective life of our people anchored in tradition, in mana. After centuries of layering, we are a culture that is resilient. We kanakas are an emerging blended race of those who call Hawai'i "home," *Hawai'i Nei*, regardless of where we live. This new blended race is robust and multicultural, rediscovering its roots and providing leadership that exceeds its number. We will take our presidents of the nation and university trustees, generals of our armed forces, our legislators and governors, our professionals, and our persistence as a people. Our persistence gives voice to the music of hope. It mutes the melancholic dirges of a dying race. It calls for the hope that enkindles. It is the hope of purpose that helps make things fit, *pono*. It also is the state's motto, "Ua mau ke ia oka 'aina ika pono (the wealth of the land is preserved in righteousness)." And it is embossed on the Hawai'i state seal. Through the many 'ohanas across the globe, the kanaka way of living perseveres.

Acknowledgements

My deepest gratitude goes to my sister Alice Maris Leilani Lujan Quiocho, Ed., Chair Human Development, Professor Emerita, Language and Literacy College of Education California State University San Marcus, for her knowledge of the family history and her four years of editing. Her constant encouragement and support kept me writing.

I also wish to thank Kalena Silva, Assistant Professor of Hawaiian Studies at the University of Hawaii, Hilo for his review of the use of Hawaiian language in the book.

Thanks also to Mustafah Dhada, Professor of Political Science at California State University, Bakersfield. Dhada is a long time friend and collegue who served as a reader and reviewer of the full text. My gratitude is further extended to James Pegolotti who took the time to provide me such valuable feedback on chapter one.

Finally, my everlasting gratitude to Samuel Hoolehe Lujan and Alice Pauline Ignacio Lujan who consistently told us the stories of their lives, who instilled in all of us their value of an education and a commitment to lifelong learning. This book is a tribute to how they shared themselves and their lives with all of their children, which we now pass on to our children and grandchildren.

www.ingramcontent.com/pod-product-compliance
Lightning Source LLC
Chambersburg PA
CBHW030323080526
44584CB00012B/676